Roots of the Republic

The
Chief Justices
of the
United States

VOLUME 5

George Lankevich

GROLIER EDUCATIONAL
Sherman Turnpike, Danbury, Connecticut

ROOTS OF THE REPUBLIC

Dr. Gary D. Hermalyn, Project Editor
Brother C. Edward Quinn, Consulting Editor
Professor Lloyd Ultan, Consulting Editor

Signers of the Declaration of Independence
by Brother C. Edward Quinn

Signers of the Constitution of the United States
by Brother C. Edward Quinn

The First Senate of the United States 1789-1795
by Richard Streb

The First House of Representatives and the Bill of Rights
by George Lankevich

Chief Justices of the United States
by Geroge Lankevich

Presidents of the United States
by Lloyd Ultan

Portraits, courtesy of The Supreme Court Historical Society

Published 1996 by Grolier Educational, Danbury, Connecticut
© 1996 by The Bronx County Historical Society

Set ISBN 0-7172-7608-2
Volume ISBN 0-7172-7614-7
Library of Congress number 95-082224

For information, address the publisher:
Grolier Educational, Danbury, Connecticut 06816.

Cover design by Smart Graphics
Book design by Henry C. Meyer Jr.

TABLE OF CONTENTS

ACKNOWLEDGMENTS

I am grateful to Dr. Gary D. Hermalyn, Executive Director of The Bronx County Historical Society, who offered me the opportunity to put into print my ideas about the distinguished men who have led the Supreme Court. Unlike the author, he never doubted that the volume would be completed. A special thank you goes to the boys of Avery Street, whose cooperation was significant. For their constant support and patience, I offer heartfelt thanks to my family and dedicate this volume to Christine and George, who know how they helped.

ABOUT THE AUTHOR

George John Lankevich is Professor of History at Bronx Community College, CUNY. The author of ten volumes of history, he served as the General Editor of *The Supreme Court in American Life*. The recipient of many research awards, he lives in Manhasset, Long Island.

INTRODUCTION

The Bicentennial of the United States Constitution was celebrated in 1987 with countless speeches lauding it as the oldest operating charter of government in the world. Our Constitution is, along with the Declaration of Independence, a defining document of America's character as a nation. Together, they represent the ideals of a people living under written law and for the highest human purposes. Far more than an idealistic statement of principle, however, the Constitution is a contract between the people and their government. It is a guide to the allocation of power, but like any contract, is subject to different interpretations. The American people have entrusted the final decision on those differing assessments to the panel of black robed justices who sit as the Supreme Court of the United States. It is their responsibility to interpret our revered national texts, and it does not matter to citizens that the members of the Court are unelected, have lifetime appointments, deliberate in secret and feel no obligation to explain their decision making processes. And although the people find it easy to threaten, "I'll take [my case] to the Supreme Court," they permit the Court to decide for itself what cases it will hear. All this justifies the expectation of the Founding Fathers that a national judiciary, the "least dangerous branch" of government, was the best way to protect the traditional values written into the Constitution.

At the center of the Supreme Court sits the chief justice, first among equal judges, yet always a symbol of the high bench to the nation. Sixteen men have filled that chair, and each made contributions to the growing national faith in constitutional process. The essays that follow examine the lives of these leaders, relating them to their era and the history of the Court they headed. This is not a law book, but a volume about the men who interpreted the law. Inevitably, many cases are mentioned, but they are rarely discussed in detail, for our concern is the dynamic relationship between the chief justices, their times, and the institution of the Supreme Court itself. Readers ought not to be surprised that politics, sometimes of the "hardball" variety, often appears in these essays because the national judiciary has never been divorced from reality; the leaders of the Court have included some of the best politicians America has produced. Alexis de Tocqueville, the most distinguished foreign analyst of America, remarked in 1831 that "scarcely any political question arises in the United States that is not resolved . . . into a judicial question." His insight remains true today. Although no chief justice alone can determine the law of the land, each attempts to "mass the Court" in order to make the Constitution relevant to new conditions. Each has helped to transform a practical document into an honored almost sacred, text. The Chiefs were all strong minded men who themselves disagreed on what the Constitution meant and how men ought to interpret it. But they all wished to make it "work" in the best interests of the people. It is hoped that these essays will encourage readers to further investigate the fascinating story of America's constitutional history.

CREATING THE SUPREME COURT 1787-1789

In the spring of 1787, a convention assembled in Philadelphia for the purpose of amending the existing Articles of Confederation of the United States of America. Attending delegates were authorized to alter the Articles so that they could better meet the "exigencies of the Union;" instead they became legal revolutionaries and created the Constitution. The saga of the Founding Fathers has been wonderfully told many times, most frequently by emphasizing the delegates' struggle to create a national legislature and consolidate executive power in the office of a president. Almost every citizen can recall that the men of Philadelphia, from their study of Montesquieu's writings, believed in the importance of separation of powers and that they intended to create three coequal branches of power in the new government. But the Convention's development of the third branch, the judicial power, and its authorization of a Supreme Court to interpret the new Constitution, is undoubtedly the least examined area of the process that created our nation. Yet, in many ways, the Supreme Court is the most innovative of all the institutions created by the Constitution. Understanding its origins, and considering the achievements of the men who have led the Court, can greatly enhance a citizen's enjoyment of American history.

Of the fifty-five men who occasionally attended the Constitutional Convention, thirty-four were lawyers. No group of professionals had been more identified with the revolutionary movement. No group understood so intimately that of all the inadequacies of the Articles of Confederation, most striking was its failure to create a judiciary. As a result of that oversight, many interstate squabbles had continued to fester since there was no finally determining legal power. But perhaps this was not so unusual since, at the time the Convention met, only six of the original thirteen American states had created independent judicial branches for their governments. It seemed clear that many Americans still perceived a strong judiciary as a tool of monarchy, a means whereby kings could bend the law to their purposes as the hated George III had done before 1776. Given this attitude and the character of the Convention delegates, it seems remarkable how little debate there was at Philadelphia over the concept of a separate, independent judicial branch. The original Virginia Plan, presented by Governor Edmund Randolph on May 29th, simply called for the creation of a national judiciary "to consist of one or more supreme tribunals, and of inferior tribunals to be chosen by the National Legislature." Randolph also suggested that a Council of Revision, drawing its membership from both executive and judicial branches, should be created to approve or veto legislative acts. That idea was quickly altered by the Convention since the Council would clearly violate the separation of powers. Never changed was the near unanimity that a judicial branch must be part of the emerging Constitution.

Most Americans remember that it took the Convention several months to agree on the Great Compromise regarding Congressional representation, and a few can recall that the Founding Fathers voted over twenty times before they arrived at a procedure for electing a President for the republic. The great care they took to define the powers and the prerogatives of the legislative and executive branches is proven by the length and complexity of Articles I and II of the Constitution. But Article III, which created the judicial arm is far shorter; it authorizes the least well defined branch of the new government. The delegates did not mandate any structure except for "one Supreme Court," to which they gave a severely restricted jurisdiction. Congress was empowered to "ordain and establish" inferior federal courts, if it chose to do so, and held the power to determine the size of the Supreme Court. Moreover, because of the ingrained fear of judicial abuse, Congress was granted the right to limit even the appellate jurisdiction of the new Supreme Court. Later, in Article VI, the Constitution was called "the supreme law of the Land," but nowhere did the document explicitly affirm the nature of the Court's power to interpret the Constitution. The Constitution, it appeared, would be supreme, but which branch would decide its meaning was left to the discretion of the leaders of the future.

Although it would be fifteen years before the Court fully claimed the right to decide constitutional questions by judicial review, most modern scholars believe that the men of Philadelphia did expect the Court they approved to exercise such power.

The most influential commentary on the Constitution remains *The Federalist Papers*, written by Alexander Hamilton, John Jay, and James Madison in 1788, and the concept of judicial oversight constantly recurs there. Laws and treaties, said Federalist No. 22, "are a dead letter without courts to expound and define their true meaning," and so "ought to be submitted in the last resort to one SUPREME TRIBUNAL." It was the federal courts, the authors held, which should be trusted to protect the nature of this limited Constitution; they would do so fairly since they comprised "incontestably" the weakest branch of the government. Federalist No. 78 explicitly argued that courts are "least dangerous to the political rights of the constitution" since the judiciary "has no influence over either the sword or the purse, no direction either of the strength or the wealth of society. . . . It may truly be said to have neither Force nor Will, but merely judgement." Hamilton, who wrote both essays, was aware that some Americans were apprehensive that courts and unelected judges might ultimately become the arbiters of the nation's future. But as a framer of the Constitution, and now as commentator on its meaning, he held that a strong judiciary would supervise both other branches and thirteen states limiting them to their proper constitutional spheres. The judiciary could do so morally since in terms of power it was the "least dangerous branch."

Although it is impossible today to discover exactly the expectations of the Fathers for the Supreme Court, there is no doubt that they authorized Congress to "ordain and establish" the federal judicial system. During the First Congress that task was undertaken by Senator Oliver Ellsworth of Connecticut, a man destined to later become the third chief justice. Ably seconded by William Paterson of New Jersey, who also would serve on the high bench, Ellsworth drafted the Judiciary Act of 1789, which remains the foundation of our court system. Ellsworth wrote the bill and then shepherded it to enactment past extreme nationalists and fearful states righters; "this bill is a child of his," wrote an admiring opponent, "and he defends it with the care of a parent." When signed by President George Washington on September 24th, the act established two types of lower federal courts – district courts in each state and three circuit courts with limited jurisdiction – and capped the structure with a Supreme Court consisting of "a chief justice and five associate justices." Parochial state fears of national domination were eased by permitting state courts to exercise concurrent jurisdiction in many areas. It was conceded that most cases would indeed be settled by state action.

Appeal to the Supreme Court was possible when a state court ruling seemed constitutionally suspect. The right to bring state cases on a writ of error to the Supreme Court was enacted in Section 25 of the Judiciary Act, perhaps its most famous paragraph. Congress there conceded to the Court the power to reverse or to affirm the decisions of state courts in federal matters. Not only did this assert the federal government's supremacy over states, but it was also a legislative acknowledgement that the ultimate power to decide on the constitutionality of law lay in the judicial branch. *The Federalist* had feared that the judiciary might be overpowered by the other branches of government, but Congress' legislative recognition of the Supreme Court's ultimate authority virtually guaranteed that the Founding Fathers' vision of three coequal branches would become a reality. In every decision that it has made, the Supreme Court, and the sixteen men who have led it during its two centuries of existence, has consolidated and shaped the power it was first granted in 1789. This is the story which emerges in the vignettes that follow.

THE
CHIEF JUSTICES
OF THE
UNITED STATES

JOHN JAY

December 12, 1745 - May 17, 1829

Chief Justice: September 26, 1789 - June 29, 1795

The task of organizing institutions is the most difficult challenge faced by any new government. George Washington, therefore, has always been honored as the leader whose integrity and wisdom established the American presidency on a firm foundation; he created executive precedents which endure to this day. Far less known is the development of our Supreme Court; yet Washington himself called the judiciary "the chief pillar upon which our national Government must rest." To lead that branch of the republic, Washington selected a man whose appointment would be "a grateful thing to the good citizens of the United States." John Jay of New York was a forty-five year old lawyer who had already contributed fifteen years of virtually uninterrupted service to the emerging nation. Although Jay is today one of the lesser known of the Founding Fathers, few of his contemporaries served the United States in as many capacities or performed them so admirably as did this gentleman from Westchester County. Jay organized the first Supreme Court and led the institution as it began to carve itself a role in American life. As the first Chief Justice of the United States, he led a court without precedents, customs, chambers, or settled law, yet provided it with enough of his own prestige and character to set it firmly into the fabric of the republic.

John Jay, the sixth son of a prosperous New York City merchant, was born in Manhattan on December 12, 1745. His boyhood was spent largely on the family estates in Rye near Long Island Sound, north of what later became The Bronx. Classically educated, he graduated from Kings College (Columbia) in 1764 and then read law in the office of Benjamin Kissam. Admitted to the New York bar in 1768, he began a successful career and was known as an "eminent barrister" by 1775. Jay always considered himself to be a conservative, yet, as revolution approached he quickly embraced the colonial cause. Before hostilities began, he served on the New York Committee of Correspondence, and, afterward, was elected to both Continental Congresses. In July of 1776, he was in New York drafting a new constitution for the rebellious province. During the bleak early years of the Revolution, Jay was one of a group of exceptional leaders who kept the state operative in the face of British invasions and the seven year occupation of New York City. Jay served as first Chief Justice of New York State (1777 - 1778) and issued the first interpretations of the constitution he had written. When, in 1778, he rejoined the Continental Congress, the representatives named him their president. Since he was willing to serve in any capacity, Congress appointed Jay ambassador to Spain on September 27, 1779, and he left soon thereafter to represent American interests in Madrid.

During the decade 1779 to 1789, Jay's major preoccupation was not law, but the foreign affairs of his struggling nation. As ambassador to Spain he secured both arms and money for the patriot cause, but failed in his goal of achieving full diplomatic recognition. As he gained experience, he came to understand that the national goals of Spain and its ally, France, did not always coincide with those of the United States. In the spring of 1782, he joined with John Adams and Benjamin Franklin to create the diplomatic team that would negotiate American independence from Great Britain. It was primarily due to Jay's mistrust of France, and his well timed withdrawal of America's demand that Britain cede Canada, that the negotiations were successful and the Treaty of Paris was signed. Even before his triumphant return to this country, Jay was appointed Secretary of Foreign Affairs for the Confederation. He held the position until 1789, but keenly felt that the weakness of the government prevented him from achieving diplomatic success. Indeed, he wrote to Thomas Jefferson that the Articles themselves were "fundamentally wrong." His duties combined with local New York politics to keep him from the Philadelphia Convention, but he approved of its goal, and quickly agreed to help write *The Federalist Papers* in defense of the Constitution. Illness limited that contribution to only five papers, but, afterward, he joined Alexander Hamilton in the memorable battle to secure New York's ratification. Jay's *Address to the People of the State of New York on the Subject of the Constitution* in April, 1788, is credited with changing the minds of several Anti-Federalists; at the Poughkeepsie Convention he and Hamilton combined to bring New York into the Union as its "Eleventh Pillar."

Jay's talents were distinguished, and it was inevitable that he would be enlisted to serve the new nation. Frustrated with diplomacy, Jay rejected the post of Secretary of State, but President Washington prevailed on him to accept appointment as first chief justice; Congress approved the nomination on September 26, 1789, only two days after the presidential announcement. As he prepared to lead the third branch of government, Jay actually continued to serve as foreign secretary because Thomas Jefferson had not yet returned from France to assume the post. Not until February 1, 1790, did the Supreme Court convene for the first time, in New York City, and then it found there was little to do. Only four of the six justices attended, there were no cases, and after naming a clerk and admitting several lawyers to practice, the Court adjourned for six months. During those months, Jay's expertise was constantly used by Washington. In Chief Justice Warren Burger's delicate phrase, "Jay gave advice to Washington over the dinner table" in a fashion that would be deemed improper today. Yet in the chaos of organizing the nation, there were as yet no established boundaries between the branches, and Jay longed to be of service to his country. The Court, whose August, 1790, session lasted only two days, hardly tested his ability to contribute.

Unfortunately, during Jay's six years as chief justice, there was little for the Supreme Court to do; he and his associates made a national impact primarily by riding to their circuit courts. Under the Judiciary Act, Supreme Court justices sat with district judges to form circuit courts in the states; in theory, each high court justice had to cover a third of the nation twice a year. Jay spoke for all his colleagues when he bitterly complained of the physical burdens of "riding the circuit," yet patriotically tried to convince himself that continuous horseback riding might have some medical advantage.

While on his Northern Circuit duty, Jay first delivered opinions that helped to define the role of courts in America. In May, 1791, he held invalid a Connecticut law which violated the terms of the Treaty of Paris, and in June, 1792, his circuit court in Rhode Island unanimously voided a state law which impaired the obligation of contracts. Jay long had defended the independence of the judiciary as a separate branch. Writing for the Court, he rejected as improper a Congressional demand that Supreme Court justices sit as commissioners to examine pension applications made by Revolutionary War veterans (April, 1792). Moreover, Jay, who so freely gave personal advice to Washington, rejected the President's request that the Court provide him with legal advisory opinions. The chief justice informed Washington that no advice was possible since there was no specific case before his Court, and that the President ought to turn for counsel to his department heads. Thus, by a series of small, but cumulative acts, and in the absence of actual Supreme Court rulings, Jay helped to establish the independence of the judiciary and the primacy of federal law.

Jay's Supreme Court delivered its first major ruling, *Chisholm v. Georgia,* on February 18, 1793. Reading Article III of the Constitution literally, the Court declared that a South Carolina citizen had the right to sue the state of Georgia in the Supreme Court. Georgia rejected the decision as an invasion of its sovereignty; other states saw the ruling as a threat to economic stability; and still others felt the ruling ignored promises made by Federalists during the ratification struggle. The ruling never went into effect, and the decision led to the passage of the Eleventh Amendment (1798). But at least cases were now coming to his bench, and, in *Glass v. The Sloop Betsey* (1794), Jay led a unanimous Court in affirming American jurisdiction over prize ships and declaring illegal all prize courts established by French consuls in this country. Such opportunities to assert national sovereignty were rare during Jay's tenure.

Clearly, the chief justice chaffed at the paucity of Court business and so never ended his commitment to political affairs. In 1792, finding his Court work "intolerable," he permitted his name to be presented as a candidate for governor of New York and, although he did not campaign, only a fraudulent count defeated him. Still serving the President in foreign policy, Jay helped compose the Proclamation of Neutrality in 1793. When European disputes threatened to pull America into war, President Washington asked Jay to undertake a mission as special ambassador to Great Britain. Although Jay did not resign as chief justice, he accepted the post and left for London; he never participated in Court affairs again. While in Europe, he again was nominated for the New York governorship and was this time elected. He resigned as chief justice on June 29, 1795, and began six years as leader of his home state.

It seems clear that Jay had ambivalent feelings about the Court he led. A political man who loved activity, he found the pace of judicial life frustrating. He knew that the Court was not a policy making body and had come to hate the travelling that circuit duty imposed. Significantly, when President John Adams re-nominated him as chief justice and Congress endorsed him in 1800, Jay refused to serve. He wrote sadly that the Court lacked "the energy, weight and dignity" essential to its success; he chose instead to retire to his country estate at Katonah. Modern visitors to the Jay Homestead, a historic site on Route 22 in Westchester County, see it as it appeared in 1801 when the former chief justice took up residence. Jay had hoped to live there with his wife, Sarah Livingston, but her untimely death made his retirement years long and lonely. His last public service was to act as president of the American Bible Society in 1821. He died in Bedford, New York, on May 17, 1829.

JOHN RUTLEDGE
September, 1739 - July 18, 1800

Acting Chief Justice: July 1, 1795 - December 15, 1795

John Rutledge's place in American history is a substantial one, but his reputation is not due to his career on the Supreme Court. Although he was one of five men who served as both associate and chief justice, his output as a judge consists of less than five pages of opinions and his impact on the Court was negligible. Nominally a Federalist, his heart seems to have belonged to the state of South Carolina, which he often called "my country," rather than to the national government that he served only as a means to further his reputation and career. He was the first justice to resign, and the only nominee for chief justice that the Senate found unacceptable. His real contributions to America were made before his service on the Supreme Court.

Born in September, 1739 in Charleston, Rutledge belonged to an elite aristocratic class which took its leadership role for granted. The son of a doctor, Rutledge was well educated and studied law both in Carolina and at the Middle Temple, London, where he was admitted to the bar in February, 1760. On his return from England, he was elected to the assembly, where he served until the Revolution. Indeed, Rutledge held high public office for virtually his entire adult life and even came to see it as his right. Though only in his twenties, Rutledge dominated the bar and politics of South Carolina, but one historian notes that "the competition was small." His marriage to Elizabeth Grimke in 1763 produced ten children, and she provided him with domestic serenity whenever he needed a respite from politics. In 1765, Rutledge was the youngest delegate at the Stamp Act Congress and drafted the respectful memorial it presented to the House of Lords. Because Rutledge loved British law and government and hoped for reconciliation, he was always regarded with some suspicion by South Carolina radicals. Even as the leader of the state delegation to the First Continental Congress, Rutledge counseled moderation and supported proposals for accommodation with England. John Adams found in Rutledge "nothing of the profound, sagacious, brilliant, or sparkling," but that opinion was jaundiced because the South Carolinian so tenaciously defended the economic interests of his colony and his class.

Although he won election to the Second Continental Congress, Rutledge was soon called back to reorganize South Carolina's government as a member of the Committee of Safety. When the assembly met, it chose him first president of the new state. President Rutledge received the rather enormous salary of £9,000 a year, but his abilities and vigor were well worth that sum. When Britain attacked Charleston in June, 1776, Rutledge's decision to defend Fort Moultrie led to the first substantial American victory in the South. Yet some seriously questioned his commitment to the American cause after he vetoed a democratic revision of the state's constitution; democracy itself, he wrote in 1778, has defects that are "arbitrary, severe, and destructive." His opponents called him "Dictator John," and a few suspected that he entertained thoughts of offering South Carolina's neutrality to the British. Yet, after Charleston fell, Rutledge became the very spirit of rebellion. For two years, he used his absolute authority and every military means available to harry the British invaders. He retired as governor on January 29, 1781, and served successively in the South Carolina Assembly (1781-82), the Articles of Confederation Congress (1782-83), and as chief judge of the state's first court of chancery in 1784. In the latter post, Rutledge accomplished the unprecedented feat of clearing all cases from the docket. Efficient and able, Rutledge continued to believe that government by the wealthy and talented would benefit his entire state.

When South Carolina chose its delegation to the Philadelphia Convention, Rutledge led the list. "The proudest and most imperious man in the United States," he played a prominent role from the start, working to create a government not directly ruled by the people. He favored a President named by Congress and a Congress named by the legislatures, yet served as the South Carolina member of the committee which created the "Great Compromise." In order to protect slavery in the South, Rutledge insisted on the three-fifths compromise; he personally owned twenty-six slaves. Rutledge's localism was also apparent in his reluctant acceptance of the idea that federal inferior courts must be permitted to function within the states. Yet, at the same time, he supported broad powers for the national government and was himself the author of the "supremacy clause." As chairman of the Committee of Detail, he has perhaps been given too much credit for the final draft of the Constitution, but he did sign and fully endorse the document. As a member of South Carolina's ratification convention, Rutledge passionately defended the new frame of government and succeeded, on May 23, 1788, in obtaining approval for the Constitution.

In 1788, Rutledge's many services were honored by his state when it cast electoral votes for him as Vice-President. After John Adams won that post, Rutledge hoped to become chief justice and permitted his friends to lobby on his behalf. When President Washington, though well aware of Rutledge's talent and ambition, instead offered the post to Jay of New York, the South Carolinian was bitterly disappointed. Although he became senior associate justice, Rutledge never really accepted his subordinate position and did not go north to sit with the full Court during its first four sessions. He did, however, ride the Southern Circuit for two years. In another indication of the Court's meager prestige, in March of 1791, Rutledge resigned as associate justice to become chief justice of the South Carolina Court of Common Pleas. While serving there for four years, he lost his wife (1792) and encountered severe financial reverses. Therefore, when Jay was elected governor of New York, he solicited Washington to appoint him chief justice as a "more respectable and honorable" post. Washington seemed quite happy to tender him the appointment on July 1, 1795, and Rutledge prepared to preside over the August term of the Supreme Court.

The summer of 1795, however, witnessed a great national debate on the merits of the treaty that Jay had negotiated with England and which the Senate had only narrowly approved. Rutledge, who had been out of touch with national events for years, most probably did not understand the president's need to have a treaty which would prevent war with England. Moreover, since the death of his wife, he had displayed symptoms of mental illness. In any event, the newly appointed Chief Justice of the United States seemed to see the Jay Treaty only from the viewpoint of his state, and not as the current test of Federalism. At a meeting in St. Michael's Church on July 16, Rutledge roundly condemned the treaty as "prostitution of the dearest rights of free men" and particularly took notice of its deleterious impact on South Carolina's trade. The Senate had been out of session when Washington named Rutledge chief justice and, therefore, he held only a recess appointment to the Court. Accordingly, when he arrived in Philadelphia in August, he was duly sworn in and then presided over a brief Court term dealing primarily with admiralty cases; he also participated in two decisions defining the issue of expatriation, writing that "a man may . . . enjoy the rights of citizenship under two governments."

While riding circuit that fall, Rutledge became ill and returned to his Charleston home. While recovering, he was informed that the Federalist Senate, outraged by his attack on the Jay Treaty, had by a vote of ten to fourteen rejected his elevation to chief justice; he thus became the first judicial nominee not to be confirmed. His mental state had been unstable for several years, and there is some evidence that he attempted suicide on December 26th. Rutledge became an eccentric recluse for the rest of his life, though charges that he was insane seem unjustified. He died in July, 1800, and was buried in the cemetery of the church in which he delivered the speech that destroyed his public career.

OLIVER ELLSWORTH
April 29, 1745 - November 26, 1807
Chief Justice: March 4, 1796 - September 30, 1800

The Senate's rejection of John Rutledge as chief justice forced Washington to make his eleventh, and last, selection for the Supreme Court. His first inclination was to elevate Associate Justice William Cushing, but that jurist declined the honor because of his age; amazingly Cushing then served on the Court another fourteen years. Washington then turned to Oliver Ellsworth, a staunch Federalist and the influential Senator who had drafted the Judiciary Act. Long a dominant figure in Connecticut legal circles, Ellsworth's commitment to Federalism was unquestionable and he had loyally cast one of the negative votes against Rutledge. The Senators received the President's new nomination on March 3, 1796, confirmed their colleague the next day, and he assumed the chief justice's chair on March 8th. Despite great expectations, Ellsworth's career on the high bench would be brief and his accomplishments there were few when compared with his previous success.

Oliver, the second son of Captain David Ellsworth of Windsor, Connecticut, was born on April 29, 1745, by which time the family had already been in the New World for a century. His military hero father hoped that Oliver would enter the ministry, and had him privately tutored by a local Calvinist preacher until the boy entered Yale in 1762. There is a tradition which claims that Yale dismissed Ellsworth because he played pranks, but, for whatever reason, he left school and obtained his bachelor's degree from Princeton. He married Abigail Wolcott in 1771, and seven of their children survived into adulthood in the Nutmeg State. Interestingly, Ellsworth always retained a Connecticut man's love for Yale, since he sent his sons there and proudly accepted an LL.D from the school in 1790. But, in the years after his graduation, the degree was of little use as he struggled to make a living by operating a farm; he also cut wood and sold it by the cord while he labored at reading law. His persistence was rewarded when he was admitted to legal practice in 1771, and began his slow rise to prominence. One historian writes that Ellsworth earned only three Connecticut pounds in his first three years of practice, and that he often walked the twenty mile round trip to Hartford when court was in session. Such dedication was rewarded in 1774 when his Windsor neighbors made him their representative to the General Assembly and launched his public career. During the Revolutionary years, he performed admirably in a myriad of state offices even as his law practice grew phenomenally. He served as member of the Continental Congress from 1777 to 1783 and, by the end of the Revolution, he was both rich and the leading patriot legal figure in the state.

Ellsworth's judicial career began as a member of Congress' committee to adjudicate admiralty appeal cases. In 1785, he was appointed to Connecticut's Supreme Court of Errors, but soon moved to the superior court where he made a reputation as a judge of commanding presence, terse decisions, and conservative views. Inevitably, he was chosen as one of Connecticut's three representatives to the Philadelphia Convention, where he played an important role. Ellsworth is credited with being the first delegate to designate the evolving Constitution as "the government of the United States" and was co-author of the Great Compromise on representation. He served on the committee which drafted the first version of the Constitution, but, because he returned to Connecticut to perform his judicial duties, he did not sign the final document. There was no doubt of his commitment to the Constitution, however, and during Connecticut's ratification struggle, Ellsworth advocated its adoption both in print (*Letters of a Landholder*) and as a representative to the Hartford ratification convention. Indeed, during Connecticut's debate, Ellsworth specifically endorsed the idea of judicial review of legislation. His support for the new nation and his statewide prominence made his selection as senator in the First Congress almost predictable.

As Connecticut's senator from 1789 to 1796, Ellsworth performed magnificently. He had a judge's mastery of procedure, and drew up the first set of Senate Rules. He worked on the bills that organized the U. S. Army, the postal system, the consular services, and the first census. Tall and handsome, a good conversationalist and finely attired, he also excelled in conference and represented the Senate on the committee that produced the Bill of Rights. He helped write the legislation which permitted North Carolina to join the Union, and it was his suggested economic boycott that brought Rhode Island in as well. But, above all, he was responsible for the Judiciary Act (September, 1789) which organized the third branch of the new government. For years he was recognized as the spokesman for the Federalist Senate, and still ranks as one of the most influential legislators in American history. His strength and integrity, according to Vice President John Adams, made him the "firmest pillar" of the Washington administration and explains why Federalists found him so suitable for leadership of the Supreme Court.

Ellsworth joined the Court with more experience as a lawyer and politician than as a judge. The advocacy talents which he used so well in the Senate were of little use on the bench, and Ellsworth, who did not like to write, found himself somewhat awed by the strong personalities and facile pens of Justices James Wilson and Samuel Chase. Moreover, since he had joined the Court too late to hear arguments in the *Hylton* proceedings of February, 1796, he did not participate in either of the two most nationalistic decisions of the year. During the August term, however, he did lead the justices through a series of important admiralty decisions. *United States v. La Vengeance* extended the maritime jurisdiction of the nation, while *Moodie v. The Ship Phoebe Ann* again asserted the primacy of national treaty obligations. Moreover, Ellsworth rendered the Court's decision in *Wiscart v. Dauchy,* an important procedural ruling which concerned the manner in which cases could come to the high bench. As chief justice, he retained his public prominence, even receiving eleven electoral votes for president in 1796, and seemed to be assuming the Court leadership expected of him.

The years 1797 to 1799 were dull ones at the Supreme Court. While performing circuit duty, Ellsworth delivered several decisions supporting national authority (*United States v. Pardon Smith, Hamilton v. Eaton*), but he also suffered greatly from the incessant pressure of travelling. After the Eleventh Amendment won approval on January 8, 1798, Ellworth's Court unanimously found it to be legally adopted and that the Supreme Court no longer held jurisdiction when a citizen of one state sued another sovereign state. His court also seemed to defer to state pride when, in *Calder v. Bull* (1798), it validated Connecticut's belief that *ex post facto* laws applied only in criminal proceedings. The last case in which Ellsworth participated was *Turner v. Bank of North America,* and there he agreed that circuit courts held only "limited jurisdiction" and that Congress could constitutionally regulate the appellate jurisdiction of lower federal courts. During his almost three years on the bench, Ellsworth wrote only a dozen opinions and displayed a nationalistic bent, but he never really advanced the court's role as a determining factor in governmental affairs.

As a political man, Ellsworth was aware that the greatest issue facing the Adams administration was a slow drift toward war with France over commerce. By early 1799, such a conflict seemed unavoidable, yet the president determined to make one last effort to avoid war. In late February, he prevailed on his chief justice to lead a diplomatic mission to Paris. Extreme Federalists condemned the effort as cowardly, while Republicans saw the selection of Ellsworth as improper, even a "prostitution" of the judicial system. Ellsworth himself appears to have dreaded the assignment. Yet he left the Court, and did negotiate a treaty ending America's alliance with France, which also put an end to French raids on American shipping. Most historical writers, even while conceding the relative weakness of the early Supreme Court, have found the willingness of Chief Justices Jay and Ellsworth to accept diplomatic assignments to be highly improper. Chief Justice Harlan Stone, writing in 1942, asserted that "both men failed in the obligation of their office," adding "it is not by mere chance that every Chief Justice since has confined his activities strictly to his judicial duties." In personal terms, the arduous trip to France and his diplomatic chores so shattered Ellsworth's health that he decided to leave the Court. On September 30, 1800, he wrote the president of his intention to resign so that a new Federalist might be appointed to lead the highest court. Ellsworth lived on for seven years as an eccentric first citizen of Connecticut, addicted to snuff, writing excellent letters on farming methods to local newspapers, and happily studying theology. Chronic ill health plagued him, and he died in Windsor, the town where he was born, on November 26, 1807.

JOHN MARSHALL
September 24, 1755 - July 6, 1835
Chief Justice: January 27, 1801 - July 6, 1835

John Adams, whose services to the American nation are as many and varied as those of any Founding Father, wrote in 1826 that he considered his "gift" of John Marshall to the United States to be "the proudest act" of his long life. Adams had every right to be elated, and history endorses his analysis, for by virtually any standard of judgment Marshall ranks as the greatest of all chief justices. Marshall raised the struggling Court to the equal status envisioned by the Founding Fathers, and his three decades on the bench implanted a nationalistic spirit into the Constitution. Marshall was the first Cabinet officer to serve on the Court, and established a longevity record for chief justices that lasts to the present. His will and personality are so dominant in the constitutional history of the United States that they mock his pious preachment that judicial power "has no existence. Courts are the mere instruments of the law, and can will nothing." No single man contributed more to the institutional history of the Court, and few as successfully countered the localism that often threatened American unity. Yet, this paragon came to lead the Court by chance and, if truth be told, hardly seemed a suitable choice for a judicial career.

John Marshall was born in northern Virginia on September 24, 1755. He was the eldest of fifteen children, and could assert with more truth than most politicians that he was born in a log cabin, raised in rural crudity, and tempered by hard, manual labor. His formal education was slight, only a year of classical study and some private tutoring, but his father, who was an ambitious landholder and minor politician, is known to have owned a four volume set of Blackstone's *Commentaries*, which young John mastered. Thomas Marshall made himself into one of the largest landholders in his section of Virginia by the time of the Revolution, and his son was at least educated enough to rise in the participatory politics of colonial America.

When the Revolution broke out, both Marshalls supported the independence movement and joined in Virginia's expulsion of the royal governor. John served as a first lieutenant in the battle of Great Bridge in December, 1775, before joining the newly formed Continental Army. He participated in many battles, endured the hardships of Valley Forge, and won a reputation as a caring officer – his men called him "Silverheels" because he usually beat them in races. In 1779, the young veteran began the study of law at William and Mary College; for three months, he attended lectures by George Wythe and absorbed the only legal training he ever had. He won admission to the Virginia bar in 1780, was demobilized with the rank of captain, and married Mary Willis Ambler in January, 1783; their union produced ten children. Marshall's love for his

"Polly" and the tender care he provided during her chronic illnesses, comprise one of the most touching stories in all American history.

During the 1780s, Marshall built a successful law practice and held a series of local political offices. Personally charming and refreshingly down-to-earth, he was prominent enough to assume Edward Randolph's law practice when the latter became governor. When Randolph, James Madison, and George Washington (termed by Marshall the "greatest man on earth") went off to Philadelphia to write a Constitution, Marshall endorsed their efforts and, as a member of the House of Delegates, advocated adoption. During the ratification struggle in the Old Dominion, Marshall also strongly favored the idea of judicial review of legislation. His nationalistic point of view made clear his preference for the emerging Federalist Party.

In the 1790s, Marshall continued to build a fine legal reputation. He also made money by speculating in the assumed debt of Virginia, involved himself in a land venture that blighted his later finances, and turned down several offers to join Washington's administration. In 1796, he made an appearance before the Supreme Court, arguing in favor of Virginia debtors in *Ware v. Hylton,* but lost the case. Only in 1797 did he accept a government appointment, one carrying a high stipend, when he agreed to serve as one of President Adams' peace envoys to France. In what became known as the XYZ Affair, the commissioners were offered bribes, and Marshall's scornful rejection of that insult to American honor made him a national hero. Marshall rejected an appointment to the Supreme Court in September, 1798, but won election to the House of Representatives that fall. The president soon prevailed on him to become secretary of state, and it was Marshall's pleasure to receive the Ellsworth mission when it returned with an agreement that kept the peace with France. As Ellsworth desired to leave the Court, the president once again offered the post of chief justice to John Jay who refused. President Adams believed it imperative that a Federalist chief justice be named because the Republican Party had won the elections of 1800 and the judiciary suddenly was the only branch of government that might uphold party principles. The president considered elevating Justices William Cushing or William Paterson, but the former was too old and the latter too closely identified with the Hamilton faction of the party. By chance, Marshall was with Adams when Jay's formal letter of refusal was received and the issue of chief justice was settled immediately by a question and an acceptance. Marshall's nomination was sent to the Senate on January 20, 1801, and approved January 27th. On February 4, 1801, Marshall assumed the chair of the chief justice which he would occupy for thirty-four years.

Unlike his three predecessors, Marshall had no judicial experience. Those men had failed to achieve for the Court any substantive position in American life, but he was determined to surpass them and transform the judiciary into the coequal bench of government envisioned by the Fathers. As chief justice this very likeable, ill-attired country lawyer was revealed as a man of steely principle whose decisions would determine the course of national development. At first, the work of his Court remained minimal, but Marshall became its sole voice; from 1801 to 1805, the Court heard only 26 cases, but the chief justice wrote every opinion without a dissent from any justice. One of those cases, *Marbury v. Madison,* established the principle of judicial review that made the Supreme Court the final arbiter of the Constitution. The Court, until 1804, consisted completely of Federalist justices, but Marshall's control of his brethren was still extraordinary. When a newly appointed justice dared to dissent, he "heard nothing but lectures on the indecency of judges cutting at each other" for the rest of the term. Since no justice yet lived in the capital, Marshall persuaded them all to room in the same boarding house. The Court became an extended family, with judges trading stories, comparing their children, and ultimately working out opinions together. Marshall got his colleagues to agree to replace colored robes with a uniform black and to abandon individual opinions delivered *ad seriatim* in favor of a single decision for the Court. Many Democratic judges later joined his Court, but the jovial and witty Marshall remained "King of the Cloister," and almost always had his way. He remained incontestably the hardest worker among the justices, and of 1,106 full opinions delivered by his Court, he wrote 519. Of 62 cases in which the meaning of the Constitution was discussed, he wrote 36. Even more amazing was that Marshall found it necessary to dissent only nine times in 34 years. He was the "Chief" whose will determined the view of the bench. In the words of Chief Justice William Rehnquist, Marshall possessed "the power of clear statement in spades."

What were the principles that Marshall saw in the Constitution and incorporated into the law of his nation? Once he had achieved supremacy for the judiciary via *Marbury,* Marshall used the Court's power not to confront Congress, but rather to reduce the power of the states. He saw the theory of state sovereignty as dangerous to the Union, and, as early as 1809, his decision in *United States v.*

Peters made clear that no state could defy the judgment of a national court. In a long series of decisions over many years, Marshall's Supreme Court forced state after state to bow to the authority of the central government. Specifics always varied as did the reasoning, but in cases such as *Fletcher v. Peck* (1810), *Dartmouth College v. Woodward* (1819), *Cohens v. Virginia* (1821) and *Gibbons v. Ogden* (1824), states from Georgia to New York were forced to bow to federal power. Perhaps no case was as influential as *McCulloch v. Maryland* (1819) in which Marshall upheld the constitutionality of the Second Bank of the United States. Maryland's attempt to tax the federally chartered bank was illegitimate because, even though the power to tax was a concurrent power, "the power to tax involves the power to destroy." Since laws enacted by Con-gress are superior to those of the states, Maryland's tax statute was void when set against the federal authority to charter a bank. By broadly reading the "elastic clause" and the commerce clause of the Constitution, Marshall consistently expanded national power. Marshall's opinions also systematically protected property rights and contractual obligation against infringement by government or individuals.

He desired strong national power, but Marshall never lost his generation's fear that a too powerful government might compromise individual liberty. He presided over the treason trial of Aaron Burr in 1807, and, by strictly interpreting the treason clause of the Constitution, freed Burr against the wishes of President Thomas Jefferson. Jefferson never forgave Marshall, and, in 1820, was still denouncing "a crafty chief judge, who sophisticates the law to his mind." In other spheres as well, Marshall demonstrated the ambivalences of his age. The chief justice was a slave owner, but his opinions did recognize Blacks as human beings and not simply chattel; he was also a member of the American Colonization Society. The oppression of native Americans by individuals and states was considered by Marshall to be "a deep stain on the American character," and he tried to uphold the rights of the Cherokee nation in *Worcester v. Georgia* (1832). Supposedly, President Andrew Jackson was so infuriated by the decision he said "let John Marshall enforce it." Georgia did ultimately pardon Worcester, and a truce was effected between executive and judicial leaders, but the case illustrated the virtual impotence of the Court should its moral authority be flouted.

By the early 1830s, Marshall was almost despondent when he reviewed his life's work and wrote to Justice Joseph Strong that he feared "our Constitution cannot last." He was in failing health, and devastated by the death of his wife on Christmas Day, 1831. His last major decision, *Barron v. Baltimore* (1833), seems uncharacteristically weak, since it decided the Bill of Rights applied only the national government and not the states. His liver was diseased and his spine injured in a stagecoach accident, but he still hoped to outlive Jackson's administration and so guarantee that his seat would be filled by a philosophically compatible appointee. That hope was unfulfilled since Marshall's life ended on July 6, 1835. Almost symbolically, the Liberty Bell in Philadelphia cracked as it tolled in mourning. Though Marshall died with a sense of failure, the truth was that his tenure lifted the Court from obscurity and gave it a vital role in American life. The Constitution he feared for was firmly in place as the supreme law of a united nation. The country marked his passing with appropriate ceremonies, but, in the words of Justice Joseph Story, his life was his "own best eulogy."

ROGER BROOKE TANEY
March 17, 1777 - October 12, 1864
Chief Justice: March 15, 1836 - October 12, 1864

The death of John Marshall left a seemingly unbridgeable chasm in American jurisprudence. Within years, he was virtually beatified as lawyers, people, and even politicians came to recognize his greatness. Any successor would have labored under grave difficulties, and the historical reputation of Roger Brooke Taney was long obscured by the shadow of his distinguished predecessor. Yet, Taney's own contributions to the life of the law in the American nation were great and have won increasing recognition from respectful scholars. With a chief's tenure on the high court second only to Marshall's, with strength of character and subtlety of mind worthy of the Virginian, with a purity of intent that let him assert openly that being chief justice was "all that I ever desired," Taney may well rank second only to Marshall as a leader of the court. His destiny was to consolidate and to strengthen the accomplishments of the Marshall Court and to recognize wider authority in the still sovereign American states. Taney believed deeply in property rights, but also made the welfare of the people an object of legal concern. His career on the Court began and ended in controversy, but there can be no doubt that he deserves to rank among the giants of the bench.

Like Marshall, Roger Brooke Taney was a son of the South, but he came from a more privileged background. He was born, March 17, 1777, on a tobacco plantation that his family owned in Calvert County, Maryland. The first Taney in America had been an indentured servant, but the family was now land rich and socially prominent. Quite unusual was the family's Catholicism, and Taney would ultimately be the first member of that religion to serve on the Supreme Court. The young man was privately tutored, graduated first in his class at Dickinson College, and decided to enter the legal profession. He read law in the office of a local judge and quickly won admission to the bar he would brilliantly grace. In 1806, he made what proved a happy marriage to Anne Key, a sister of Francis Scott Key, and gradually built one of the largest law practices in Maryland to support a family of six lively daughters. His early Federalism gradually altered itself to support Jeffersonian principles, and he had success in local politics. He was a Jacksonian Democrat even before serving as Maryland's Attorney General from 1826 to 1831, and ran the Democratic state campaign in 1828. After a major shake-up in Jackson's Cabinet in 1831, this Catholic slaveholding Democrat became Attorney General of the United States.

Taney was fifty-four years old when he became attorney general, a lawyer who presumably had reached the pinnacle of his career. He was intensely loyal to Jackson, and provided legal opinions justifying the Administration's policy of Indian removal. In 1832, he helped draft the demagogic veto message in which the president denied recharter to the Second Bank of the United States, and, thereafter, served as Democratic "point man" in the "Bank War." After two successive Secretaries of the Treasury refused to remove federal deposits from the United States Bank, Jackson nominated Taney to the post and funds soon began to flow into "pet" banks across the country. Once, as a lawyer before Marshall's Supreme Court, Taney had argued in favor of state banking freedom, so there is no reason to believe that his actions in the Bank War were those of an unprincipled hack. But his loyalty to the president ultimately drove him from Washington when an anti-Jackson Senate rejected his nomination to the Treasury. The president retaliated by naming Taney an Associate Justice of the Supreme Court, only to have an angry Senate table that nomination in 1835. Jackson was now incensed and, in an act of both scorn and loyalty, he defied the Senate and sent it Taney's nomination to replace Marshall as chief justice. Elections had somewhat altered the composition of the Senate, and Jackson's indomitable will bent several newcomers to his demand. On March 15, 1836, after a ten week debate, the Senate bowed to the president and approved Taney to fill Marshall's seat by a vote of 29-15. One Federalist icon despaired; the Court "is gone" wrote Justice Joseph Story, but instead the high bench entered a new phase of its history.

Although Taney had strong political convictions, he never attempted to radicalize the judicial branch. The Court he inherited had a majority of Democratic appointees and, with Marshall gone, the justices were looking for leadership. Taney was never able to orchestrate opinions to the same degree as his predecessor, but he did prove a worthy successor as his Court reflected the new concerns of the nation. America was changing rapidly; its industrial base was expanding while immigrants filled eastern cities and pioneers drove into southern and western lands. Symbolically, this first Democrat to lead the Supreme Court was also the first chief justice to wear the trousers of a common man under his robes. But Taney was also a landholder who had no desire to overturn the overall trend of a Federalist jurisprudence extremely protective of property rights and national power. The Taney court did demonstrate a shift in emphasis, however, and forced a greater concern for the general community and the concurrent powers of the states into America's legal practice. That shift became immediately obvious in three decisions of 1837 (*Miln, Briscoe, Charles River Bridge*) in which the Court moved from Marshall's predicted positions. Taney and his brethren now recognized the existence of public interests that might be best met through state action. These

decisions began the Court's gradual movement away from central-
ized power, toward recognizing a dual or divided sovereignty
between Washington and the states. Chief Justice William Rehnquist later wrote that Taney discovered in the Constitution "the
necessary authority for states to solve their own problems." Such
flexibility of approach suited the times, and *Charles River Bridge*, at
first denounced as a blow against property and contractual rights,
is now seen as a decision which fostered vast economic development. Chief Justice Taney wrote that property rights must be
"sacredly guarded," but his Court believed "that the community
also have rights, and that the happiness and well being of every citizen depends on their faithful preservation." It was a judicial philosophy which affirmed a muted national sovereignty while permitting far greater leeway to "state police power" than a Marshall
might have allowed (*Licence Cases*, 1847). The overall impact of
Taney's years on the Court were to consolidate the Court's role as
interpreter of the Constitution, but to slow the pronouncement of
new constitutional theory.

Had it not been for his Court's inability to deal with the issue of
slavery, Taney's reputation would be far higher. It is well understood that the Constitution recognized the validity of slavery in the
United States, even though the dreaded word never appeared in
that document. Taney was a southerner brought up holding slaves
and, even though he manumitted all his slaves, he never liberated
himself from the belief that American Blacks were not only "weaker
members of society" but also a "degraded class." Moreover, the
chief justice was a brilliant lawyer who believed that the judiciary
might settle the moral question of slavery in America and keep the
Union together. Never was a man more mistaken. The Court had
avoided the subject of slavery by holding that Blacks took their status from the states where they lived. *Dred Scott* was a test case
meant to challenge that assertion and force the Court to discuss the
issue of slavery. It is one of the most complex decisions in legal history, all nine judges delivered opinions, but the focus of the case
has always been Taney's majority statement. It held that, following
the "intent" of the Founding Fathers, slaves were non-citizens,
could never be citizens and so had no status in federal courts.
Moreover, for the first time since *Marbury*, the Court challenged
Congress. The Missouri Compromise legislation of 1821 was
declared to be unconstitutional since it excluded slaves (property)
from territories of the United States. Taney's decision in *Dred Scott*
wandered far beyond the main issues in the mistaken belief that a
judicial statement by the Court could settle the nation's most divi-
sive moral dilemma. The need to speak with the authority of the

Court was indeed forced upon Taney by others, but he clearly believed the Court's pronouncement could halt the controversy. Instead, the case became, in the words of Chief Justice Charles Evans Hughes, a "self-inflicted wound" that almost ruined the Court and Taney in the judgement of history. Just how completely Taney misjudged the times is shown by *Ableman v. Booth* (1859), a nationalistic decision which unanimously upheld the supremacy of the federal judiciary and asserted the Supreme Court's ultimate role in determining constitutionality. Because the case involved slavery, however, northern states and popular opinion refused to accept reasoning they normally would have cheered.

When Taney swore in Lincoln as President, he heard the new executive pledge a reversal of *Dred Scott.* The Chief now was old, crushed by the loss of his wife and a daughter to yellow fever, and denounced by Republicans as a traitor. Named to the Court by a strong president, his last years were a constant battle against Lincoln's extension of presidential authority to fight the Civil War. Although Taney was the first chief justice to live in Washington, he was hardly a beloved figure on its social scene. He was not trusted, since his opinions regarding the right to habeas corpus and the legitimacy of the blockade would have made it more difficult to fight the war had they been implemented. Although he had freed his slaves, he was denounced as a rebel and was probably the only chief justice ever to be placed under federal surveillance. The Lincoln government encouraged him to resign, but he continued to serve beyond the age of eighty-seven. He died on October 12, 1864, lonely, bitter, isolated, and impotent on the Court he had once dominated.

SALMON PORTLAND CHASE
January 13, 1808 - May 7, 1873
Chief Justice: December 6, 1864 - May 7, 1873

During the Civil War, leadership of the nation centered on the person of Abraham Lincoln, and he vastly expanded the limits of executive power to keep the Union together and win the bloody conflict. Congress generally followed the lead of the president, while Taney's judiciary was in disrepute with its integrity and loyalty suspect. As the war raged on, age began to take its toll on the Supreme Court and several associate justices died. Congress sped up the process of change by expanding the high bench to ten justices. Clearly, both president and Congress desired a more friendly Supreme Court, and the death of Taney in 1864 provided Lincoln with the opportunity to consolidate reform by naming a chief justice. But the man selected, Salmon Portland Chase, proved less than an inspired choice. He was, perhaps, the most politically oriented of all the chief justices, and, although he presided over the Supreme Court for almost nine years, he never dominated it. He always thought his proper place was in the White House. In some respects, Chase's tenure did expand the Court's authority; ten acts of Congress were found unconstitutional compared to only two such decisions in the previous seventy-five years, and he did help to rebuild the reputation of the judiciary. But in all, his regime never fully satisfied either himself or those who today assess his place in Supreme Court history.

Chase was born in Cornish, New Hampshire, on January 13, 1808, the eighth child of a tavern keeper who dabbled in local politics. His father died when he was only nine, and the youngster was sent to live with an uncle who was the Episcopal Bishop of Ohio. In Ohio, Chase developed an austere, highly moral view of life and politics; during his lifetime he would read scripture daily, never curse or play cards, and rarely laugh. As a lad, he attended church school before returning to New Hampshire, where he graduated from Dartmouth College in 1826. He lived briefly in Washington, where another uncle served as U.S. Senator, and there he ran a private boy's academy. While living in the capital city he began the study of law under the sponsorship of U.S. Attorney General William Wirt. Admitted to the bar in 1829, Chase moved to Cincinnati, where his early practice seems to have been debt collection. It was in Cincinnati, that Chase married for the first time, but Katherine Garniss died in December, 1835. His subsequent marriages to Eliza Smith (d. September 29, 1845) and Sara Dunlop (d. January 13, 1852) produced six children, but only two of them survived into adulthood.

As the years passed, Chase won a reputation as a committed abolitionist, and often acted as unpaid counsel to the anti-slavery movement. His moral outrage at the very existence of slavery made him "attorney general for runaway Negroes;" he even argued one case up to the Supreme Court. Inevitably, the young Whig was drawn into politics, and he became a leader of the Liberty Party and, subsequently, the Freesoilers. In 1849, his national political career began when the Freesoilers bartered control of the Ohio legislature in return for a Senate seat and sent Chase to Washington; his cooperation there with other anti-slavery men made him one of the founders of the Republican Party. Chase was elected the first Republican governor of Ohio in 1855, reelected in 1857, and was considered a highly competent executive. He believed that his accomplishments merited the new party's presidential nomination in 1856, but it went to General John Frémont. He was certain that he deserved it in 1860, and bitterly resented Lincoln's success. Republican victory in Ohio gave the party control of the legislature, however, and on Inauguration Day – March 4, 1861 – Chase again entered the Senate as Lincoln assumed the presidency.

As the nation plunged toward war over slavery, Chase, on March 6th, accepted the President's offer to join the Cabinet as Secretary of the Treasury. He proved an outstanding choice, raising unprecedented amounts of money via loans and bond sales, and also devising the national banking system that would endure for fifty years. Chase, who had outlived three wives, also pioneered the hiring of women by the Treasury Department. When Congress authorized the issuance of paper money notes as legal tender for the settlement of debt, Chase dubiously but loyally accepted the innovation. But he was not content as secretary; his presidential ambitions led him to serve as a rallying point for all those Republicans who found Lincoln's war management unsatisfactory. Believing himself to be irreplaceable, Chase constantly opposed the president over policy decisions and often threatened to resign. Finally, after his renomination to a second presidential term was certain, an exasperated Lincoln shocked Chase by accepting his resignation. Only Taney's death saved Chase's career because the president, anxious to placate the Radical Republicans and still respectful of Chase's abilities, nominated him chief justice; he knew Chase's positions regarding slavery, emancipation, and legal tender, and believed the former secretary would make the perfect head of a "Lincoln Court." The Senate agreed, affirmed the nomination on December 6th, the same day it was received, and gave Chase leadership of a Court whose primary task would be to deal with the meaning of the war.

Chief Justice Chase remained intensely political. The tasks of the Court were routine in the early months of 1865, but then the assassination of Lincoln stimulated Chase's always present ambition. He willingly accepted a commission from President Andrew Johnson to examine conditions in the defeated South, and happily watched as the president began to feud bitterly with the Radical Republicans in Congress over the reconstruction of the states. His sympathies were with the party that passed the Thirteenth and Fourteenth Amendments, constitutional changes which eliminated the heritage of *Dred Scott* and promised equality to 4,000,000 new citizens. Thus, while the majority of his Court rebuffed legislative pretensions to power in decisions like *Milligan* (1866) and the *Test Oath Cases* (1867), Chase joined in minority opinions supportive of Congress. And by 1867, he seemed to have convinced his brethren that they ought to stand aloof from the political elements of the reconstruction process. His personal goal remained the Republican nomination, and future Chief Justice Morrison Waite wrote: "My predecessor detracted from his fame by permitting himself to think he wanted the Presidency." Some less charitable commentators thought that ambition also influenced Chase's judicial views. But by early 1868, his party's preference for a military hero, Ulysses S. Grant, was obvious. Perhaps disappointment made Chase a better judge, for that summer, he became the only chief justice ever to preside over the impeachment trial of a president. He capably filled the role of presiding judge at Andrew Johnson's trial, insisting that courtroom procedures and rules of evidence be honored. The chief justice refused to act as a partisan, used his rulings to moderate anger, and, some Radicals believed, was responsible for the president's acquittal by the margin of a single vote. Once the trial ended, Chase – a founder of the Republican Party – permitted friends to inform the Democrats that he would accept their nomination for the Presidency. Even today it is difficult to assess which party was more outraged by his arrogance.

With most politicians and his fellow justices angered by his political maneuverings, Chase reluctantly settled into a comfortable period as chief justice. His puritan nature always made him work very hard, and he quickly wrote over 200 opinions issued by the Court. In 1869, he spoke for a unanimous Court which declared secession to be constitutionally impossible (*Texas v. White*). His political instincts remained acute, and he believed that the Court itself might become a target of Radical anger. Chase thus delayed any action in a pending case involving habeas corpus (*McCardle*) until Congress acted to deprive his Court of jurisdiction. The case remains the only instance in which Congress has made an exception to the appellate jurisdiction of the Court, a power it holds under Article III of the Constitution. Chase perhaps averted a major constitutional confrontation, since the Court's acceptance of the statute meant that it did not have to rule on the constitutionality of the Reconstruction Acts. Chase's tenure is also memorable for a major reversal in financial history when he orchestrated Court rejection of the paper money notes he had created and issued as Secretary of the Treasury. According to a later chief justice, the *Legal Tender Cases* (1870) provide a "textbook example . . . that one may look at a legal question differently as a judge" than as a politician. Those cases were complicated and controversial, and an angry Congress reacted by approving two new justices for the Court. When their votes overturned the decisions within fifteen months, both Chase and the judicial branch were humiliated.

When the reconstructed Court rejected his leadership, Chase was already weakened by the effects of a serious stroke suffered in 1870. As a result, he halved the time allocated for oral arguments before the Court, reducing it to four hours from the level authorized since 1848. His reputation for consistency was in tatters and he was too feeble to write opinions, so leadership of the Court shifted to Associate Justices Samuel Miller and Stephen Field. But in the face of political repudiation and illness, Chase still believed he could occupy the White House. In 1872, he allowed his daughter to approach both the Democratic and Liberal Republican organizations to confirm that the chief justice would accept their nomination for the Presidency; neither party seriously considered the offer. Sadly, by 1873, when the Court issued its first major pronouncement on the Fourteenth Amendment in *Slaughterhouse,* Chase was unable to prepare his own thoughts and only joined Justice Field's dissent. Clearly, his strength was waning along with his influence, and while visiting Manhattan after the term ended, he suffered another stroke. Chief Justice Chase died in New York, May 7, 1873, a man who had made great contributions to his nation, but whose personal ambition for power was his greatest weakness.

MORRISON REMICK WAITE

November 29, 1816 - March 23, 1888

Chief Justice: January 21, 1874 - March 23, 1888

The last decades of the nineteenth century saw the most profound changes in American life since the adoption of the Constitution. The revolution was economic and not political, as a
largely rural, agriculturally oriented society was transformed into a
world of cities, crowds, and industrial combinations. Chase had
once written that the Civil War created "an indestructible Union,
composed of indestructible States," and those entities were now
connected by bands of steel as an expanding railroad network tied
the continental nation together. The national government was
supreme, Court rulings from Marshall to Chase guaranteed this, but
the dynamic spirit of Gilded Age America was embodied by entre-
preneurs whose initiatives created an industrial colossus by 1900.
Steel, oil, mines, ranches, farms, factories – these were the sinews
of a suddenly gigantic America. In this new industrial society, the
task of the Supreme Court would be to define the relationship
among states, the national government, and enterprising business-
men. Property rights had always been of paramount concern to a
Court, which, almost by definition, was conservatively oriented and
staffed by men of the establishment. Morrison R. Waite, who followed Chase as chief justice, was such a person. He was a decent
and dedicated chief who grew in his new position, restored the
Court's prestige and helped create a judicial philosophy sympathetic to a businessman's America.

Morrison Remick Waite was the eldest son of a distinguished
jurist, a lawyer who served as Chief Justice of Connecticut. Born in
Lyme on November 29, 1816, Waite enjoyed the classical education
typically given to privileged young men of old New England fami-
lies. A graduate of Yale (1837) who later served on the university's
Board of Trustees, he unknowingly followed the career path of the
man who preceded him as chief justice. Like Chase, Waite went to
Ohio, read law, won admission to the bar (1839), and began to build
a practice. On September 21, 1840, Waite married his second
cousin, Amelia Warner, and the couple had five children. The young
lawyer played an active role in Whig local politics, serving in the
Ohio Assembly and on Toledo's City Council, and, like Chase,
switched his allegiance to the newly created Republican Party in
the 1850s. His ambition was the modest one of legal eminence, and
his talent and drive saw him create one of Ohio's most successful
law firms by 1860. His specialty was property law, and he num-
bered several large railroads among his extensive cliental. He supported Lincoln, mistrusted the Radicals, and stood with the conservative wing of the Republican Party during the war. He was
prominent enough to be offered a seat on Ohio's Supreme Court,
but refused the offer in favor of an advisory role to Governor John

Brough. Diligence and connections brought him wealth and, by the end of the decade, he sat on the boards of several corporations in addition to his thriving legal practice.

Waite's public career did not begin until 1871, the year he was named by President Ulysses S. Grant as one of three American commissioners who would negotiate the "Alabama claims" against Confederate wartime naval raiders constructed in Great Britain. His was a surprising selection, but he worked hard at Geneva and the settlement brought him some reflected glory, since $15,500,000 was awarded to the nation. Upon Waite's return home, both Ohio parties jointly named him a delegate to the state constitutional convention, and he was unanimously chosen its presiding officer. Waite's sudden preeminence was a godsend to the Grant administration which, since the death of Chase, had been severely embarrassed as half a dozen men had either declined to accept or failed Senate scrutiny for the post of chief justice. In January, 1874, the president surprised the nation and shocked Waite by sending his name to the Senate. Waite had never held a judicial post nor argued before the Supreme Court, and he was virtually unknown to official Washington. Yet, senators proved overjoyed to receive a practical nomination. On January 21st, after a minimum of debate and with a sense of relief, the Senate confirmed his selection by a vote of 63-0. The untested Waite immediately took charge of a Court filled with brilliant associate justices who, at first, were condescending to him. However, he soon won their respect with his modesty, tact, and enormous capacity for work. Not only did the new chief justice write over 1,000 opinions during his tenure, but also he lifted the onus of politics with which Chase had saddled the Court. Waite refused to allow his name to be used in presidential speculation, and rejected as improper his serving on the Electoral Commission named to determine the result of the disputed election of 1876. By the end of his regime, his self-effacing dignity and solid leadership of a conservative bench restored the luster of the Supreme Court.

For Americans in 1874, the Civil War was beginning to recede into history, but most citizens agreed that its fundamental meaning was codified in the three amendments to the Constitution passed from 1865 to 1870. The ostensible purpose of those measures was to guarantee equality to Black Americans. It was Waite's Court which interminably wrestled with interpreting the Fourteenth Amendment, that section of the Constitution which, a century later, has become the most litigated part of the document. The drafters of that amendment had intended to define the areas in which the defeated southern states would be obligated to protect the rights, the "privileges and immunities," of the new citizens of the United

States. The guarantees of the Bill of Rights would apply to the states as well as to the federal government. In the only previous interpretation of the amendment's meaning in the *Slaughterhouse Cases* (1873), the Chase Court had rejected this broad view of "privileges and immunities." The issue in *Slaughterhouse*, in any event, was not Black rights but Louisiana's right to grant a monopoly. Four dissenting justices believed that the Fourteenth Amendment ought to be used to protect the property rights of New Orleans butchers who claimed their substantive due process right to practice their profession was being violated. This was the legal situation existing when Waite assumed control of the Court, and his major decision in *Munn v. Illinois* (1877) affirmed that states could legitimately regulate property, in the form of rates charged by grain elevators, because sometimes it is "affected with a public interest." Many corporations argued that establishing maximum rates took away their property, the right to charge higher rates, without due process. Waite rejected this, noting only that excessive regulation might be unconstitutional if it too greatly limited a corporation's freedom to make money. His recognition that rates ought to be reasonable ultimately permitted future Courts to judge whether states or nation were denying due process of law to corporations by their economic regulations. Waite was never much of a phrasemaker, but in *Munn* he told the nation that, if faced with an abuse of legislative police power, it "must resort to the polls, not to the courts."

In 1877, the conception of due process still meant procedural rights, not substantive ones, but Waite's Court spent most of the next decade moving away from its early acceptance of state regulation. Waite was, after all, a corporate attorney concerned with encouraging business growth, and his conservative constitutional views inclined him to accept the prevailing philosophy of *laissez faire* regarding property rights. Gradually, he came to accept Justice Stephen Field's argument that the Fourteenth Amendment guaranteed the substantive due process rights of all persons, and that business corporations were "persons" in the eyes of the law. In a long series of cases, Waite and his Court moved to limit the regulatory powers of the states and to expand the substantive property rights of corporations as persons. By 1886, over Waite's dissent, the *Wabash* decision denied that any state power to regulate interstate commerce existed. In *Santa Clara* (1886), the chief justice told the litigants that his Supreme Court believed the Fourteenth Amendment forbids states to deny persons, i.e. corporations, the equal protection of the laws. The Court assumed a stance in support of property that wrote the philosophy of *laissez faire* into the Constitution for generations.

But Waite's judicial concern did not use the "privileges and immunities" clause to actively support the rights of America's Black citizens as the Radicals of wartime had expected. During the 1870s, both the executive and legislative branches abandoned their commitments to Black equality and consigned 4,000,000 new citizens to the protection of the "redeemed" Southern states. By reading the Fourteenth Amendment very narrowly, Waite's Court joined in this moral retreat and provided it with judicial sanction. The Fifteenth Amendment was interpreted not as guaranteeing the right to vote, but merely as prohibiting states, who set suffrage requirements, from discriminating on the basis of race or color. Louisiana's laws prohibiting racial segregation in transportation facilities were invalidated as an unconstitutional encroachment on the power of Congress to regulate interstate commerce. And finally, in the *Civil Rights Cases* of 1883, the justices declared that private acts of social discrimination could not be redressed by Congress, but only through state action. Waite's Court found three major civil rights laws to be unconstitutional, and permitted the South to create a system of Jim Crow segregation that imposed a second class citizenship on Blacks. The chief justice accepted this gutting of the Fourteenth Amendment's intent even though he personally advocated federal spending for Black education and worked to accomplish that end as a trustee of both the Peabody and Slater Funds. The contrast between his official and personal actions never seems to have bothered Waite.

In retrospect, Waite developed a rather consistent legal approach to the needs of an expanding America; in his pedestrian fashion, he worked hard to have the Court foster development and social stability in an industrial society. The work of the law was hard, but he never slackened the pace which made him so prolific in the writing of opinions. Moreover, he actively participated in the social life of the capital with the flair of a transplanted Ohio lawyer. His last decision, a full volume long, upheld the validity of Alexander Graham Bell's telephone patents, an endorsement of business monopoly which rang true for another century. He took ill with pneumonia after delivering the opinion, and died on March 23, 1888, after serving as chief justice for fourteen revolutionary years.

MELVILLE WESTON FULLER

February 11, 1833 - July 4, 1910

Chief Justice: July 20, 1888 - July 4, 1910

The sudden death of Chief Justice Waite provided an opportunity for President Grover Cleveland, the only Democrat to break Republican control of the White House in the last third of the century, to name a leader for the Supreme Court. Although he led the alternative party, Cleveland shared prevailing conservative attitudes toward business enterprise. The president's choice, therefore, did not represent a radical alternative to the economic verities of the age. In addition, the Philadelphia *Press* wrote that Melvin Fuller was the most obscure man ever appointed chief justice, and he may well remain so today! His Court completed the refitting of the Constitution to the altered needs of industrial America begun during Waite's tenure, and continued the virtual enshrinement of free market, *laissez faire*, capitalism. In the process it enhanced the power of the judicial branch to validate both state and federal regulatory legislation. Fuller's constitutional principles favored industry, and his Court acted as a bulwark to deflect, and even crush, radicals who would disrupt the operation of the American economy. In brief, Fuller proved far more concerned with property rights than human rights in the twenty-two years he led the Court.

Melville Weston Fuller, the son of an attorney, was born in Augusta, Maine, on February 11, 1833. His family had long been legally prominent in Maine, and the boy was actually raised by his grandfather, a judge, after his parents divorced. He graduated from Bowdoin College where he won renown as a poet, read law in the office of an uncle, attended Harvard Law School for a year, and entered the expected profession. Like many other ambitious young men, he went west and, settling in Illinois, was admitted to the bar in June, 1856. In politics the struggling young lawyer was a Douglas Democrat, and, during the Civil War, party loyalty led him to oppose many of Lincoln's policies. His failure to enlist in the army and his opposition to emancipation were remembered in 1888 and delayed his approval as chief justice. During the war, Fuller's first wife Calista Ophelia Reynolds had died, and his 1866 remarriage to Mary Coolbaugh, daughter of a wealthy banker, opened doors previously closed to him. In the short space of five years, he became one of Chicago's most successful lawyers, a fortunate occurrence since his family rapidly grew to eight children. His defense of the Reverend Charles Cheney against charges of "low church" practice gained Fuller national repute and led to the founding of the Reformed Protestant Episcopal Church. But most of his legal work consisted of real estate and commercial law, and by obtaining for Chicago the right to develop lakeshore property, he helped facilitate the creation of its park system. By the mid-1880s, Fuller's income surpassed $30,000 a year, and he was rich, happily married, and professionally respected.

Grover Cleveland first met Fuller during a presidential swing through the Midwest, and was impressed by his sound money views, low tariff stand, and loyalty to the Democratic Party. The president had already made two unsuccessful attempts to recruit Fuller into government service, and so his choice for chief justice surprised the nation. Fuller had no judicial experience and the most probable reason for his appointment was geographic, since the seventh circuit had not been represented on the Court for a decade. But Fuller's credentials were solid, and he looked the part of a judge who could capably lead America into its second century under the Constitution. After an extended debate, the Senate by a vote of 41-20 accepted the president's nominee on July 20, 1888. Although Fuller never dominated the Court in the manner of a Marshall, he proved an efficient manager and a tactful, wise, administrator. In 1891, he lobbied effectively for the passage of a bill which ended the "circuit riding" obligation of justices and established additional Courts of Appeal. He worked to achieve a collegial atmosphere on his Court, and went so far as to hold conference meetings in his home, the remodeled boarding house in which the Marshall Court had resided in the 1830s. Fuller began the now traditional practice of a judicial exchange of handshakes before conference or decision reading, and won his colleagues' respect by willingly giving up his privilege of writing important decisions. He was a tireless worker who delivered over 850 decisions in his twenty-two years on the bench, and his personal charm and lack of pretension allowed him to preside over a happy Court in a dignified manner. His refusal to become Secretary of State in a second Cleveland administration also enhanced the prestige of the Court. When the Court was offered the opportunity in 1896 to leave its cramped Capitol quarters to move into the Congressional Library, Fuller convinced the justices to remain in the old Senate Chamber because of its historic setting. Even his judicial opponents respected this Chief's operation of the Court, and Justice Oliver Wendell Holmes, certainly no legal conservative, became one of his close friends.

During the 1890s, the Supreme Court's endorsement of *laissez faire* economic theories, its reverence for private property rights, and its distrust of governmental power reached its highest levels. Fuller shared this conservative view of the Constitution, and, during his tenure, the justices methodically reversed or limited the regulatory authority of the states. At times, it seemed that lawyers merely had to assert that state law violated the due process rights of corporate "persons" in order to obtain a Supreme Court hearing and, probably, a legal victory. In large part due to Fuller, the Court regained a self-confidence it had not demonstrated for decades, and a long series of decisions made clear that the Fourteenth Amendment was the best defense of corporate enterprise. The height of this conservative reading of the Constitution may well have been 1895, a year that populist agitation and reform demands were being heard across the nation. In January, Fuller delivered the decision in *E.C. Knight*, the Court's first ruling on the Sherman Anti-Trust Act. The chief justice found that, although a sugar refining corporation controlled 95% of the supply, it remained only a manufacturer, did not engage in commerce, and so was not in restraint of trade according to the intent of the Sherman Act. In May, Fuller provided the argument whereby a 5-4 majority in *Pollock* declared the national income tax imposed in 1894 to be unconstitutional. The Court's critics argued that *Pollock* represented a surrender to the interests of the propertied classes and was a "judicial amendment of the Constitution." Nevertheless, the decision delayed imposition of a national tax until the Sixteenth Amendment was passed. Legal scholars assert that neither *Knight* nor *Pollock* were as well written or argued as they might have been, but both decisions were predictable from Fuller's Court. Equally devastating to opponents of industrial power was the Court's acceptance of federal injunction power to break the Pullman Strike of 1894. In *re Debs* declared a railroad strike illegal because it interfered with the mail, and affirmed the government's "right to apply to its own courts for any proper assistance," including federal injunctions. According to the Supreme Court, the government had no power to regulate manufacturing or to tax people, but certainly could help corporations break strikes. Finally, in a decision that endured for almost sixty years, Fuller's Court completed the abandonment of Black America by approving, in *Plessy v. Ferguson* (1896), the "separate but equal" doctrine. It is interesting to note that Fuller, like Waite before him, was an active member of the Peabody Fund during his tenure on the Court, yet fully endorsed this misguided decision.

Fuller believed the Constitution was a limited grant of power to central government and so mistrusted any expansion of federal authority. Even when Justice Holmes joined the Court in 1902 and began to issue ringing dissents against a too restrictive reading of the Constitution, Fuller's Court remained stolidly conservative. Fuller rarely had to dissent from opinions, and, in 1905, he was part of the majority which decided that New York State's attempts to protect bakery workers by limiting their work to 60 hours violated the due process clause. The *Lockner* decision was denounced by

Justice Holmes, but the Fuller Court had protected a workman's liberty of contract guaranteed by the Fourteenth Amendment. During his last years on the bench, Fuller did moderate his conservatism to a degree, at least as it applied to women laborers; the *Lockner* precedent was modified by *Muller v. Oregon* (1908) in which a unanimous Court accepted the "Brandeis Brief" on behalf of laundry workers.

In addition to his Court duties, Fuller served the nation as a member of the Venezuelan-British Guiana Border Commission (1899) and as the American representative to the Permanent Court of Arbitration at The Hague in the Netherlands. His settled view of the Constitution was not compatible with the dynamism of President Theodore Roosevelt, however, and there is some proof that White House pressure was brought to bear on Fuller to resign. The chief justice refused to cooperate with that demand and continued to attend first night theatrical performances and read the latest novels well after Roosevelt was gone. On the Fourth of July, 1910, while vacationing at his summer home in Sorrento, Maine, Fuller suffered a heart attack and died at the age of seventy-seven.

EDWARD DOUGLASS WHITE
November 3, 1845 - May 19, 1921
Chief Justice: December 12, 1910 - May 19, 1921

Edward D. White was the first Roman Catholic to sit on the Supreme Court since Roger B. Taney and, by a series of unexpected chances, followed the example of his predecessor and became chief justice. He was the first associate justice transferred to the center seat of the Court, and filled the position with wit and distinction. Naturally a judicial conservative, White never forgot that the influence of the Court he led was dependent "solely upon the approval of a free people," and his tenure reduced the rigid *laissez faire* which had characterized the bench for forty years. In his view, the Court's duty was to apply reason to the changing society of the United States, to protect the people from the dangers of unlimited power whether it came from business or the executive, and to uphold the Constitution as the finest expression of America's faith in democracy. To a very large degree he succeeded in his goals and, though a later chief justice considered him indecisive and rambling, others found that White dominated his Court quietly and kept it harmonious. All commentators agree White was an extraordinary human being and a fine colleague.

The future chief justice was born in Lafourche Parish, Louisiana, on November 3, 1845, into an Irish Catholic family. His father was a Democratic politician who served five terms in the House and one term as governor before White was even born. The young man received a Catholic education at the hands of the Jesuits, and was a student at Georgetown when the Civil War began. Leaving college, he enlisted as a Confederate private and was taken prisoner at the battle of Port Hudson; he was briefly imprisoned before being paroled for the rest of the war. Only in 1865 did he begin to read law and, after attending the state School of Law, he was admitted to Louisiana's bar in 1868. As he slowly built a practice, White also rose in Democratic political circles, and from 1878 to 1880 served as a member of the Louisiana Supreme Court. He was a recognized member of the New Orleans establishment, and ultimately was sent to the U.S. Senate because of his opposition to a corrupt state lottery. As senator, he faithfully supported his state's desire for federal sugar subsidies, an easy task since it was also in his family's economic interest. He proved so loyal to the Cleveland administration in all other matters that he became Democratic Majority Leader in 1894; that year was also marked by his marriage to Virginia Kent. His road to the Supreme Court was an unusual one, and stemmed from a feud between President Cleveland and Senator David Hill over the "New York" seat on the Court. Hill and the president found it impossible to agree on a mutually acceptable candidate for an empty justice's chair, and Hill had used "Senatorial privilege" to force the rejection of two Cleveland nominees. The enraged president then named White to the Court, ignoring New York, yet guaranteeing approval of his choice since the "courtesy" due a fellow member of the Senate came into play. White took his seat on March 12, 1894, and remained an important associate justice until he moved to the center seat in 1910.

White's fundamental legal position was a belief that state and federal powers ought to be limited, and that individual freedoms ought to be protected by the law. He was a judicial conservative who wrote that the Court ought never to declare a statute unconstitutional on the grounds that the it was "unwise or unjust" (1904), but only because it explicitly violated the words of the Constitution. He was thus a dissenter in the income tax case, but joined the Court majority in both *Knight* and *Debs* in 1895. His early opinions favored a broad reading of contractual rights, yet in *Lockner* he would have permitted the state of New York to protect individual bakers despite their "right" to accept low wages. He was not a liberal by any means, yet he did believe that state "police power" could protect individuals by establishing maximum working hours; he joined the majority in *Muller v. Oregon* (1908), where liberty of contract was restricted in order to protect the health of women workers. Associate Justice White's reputation was that of a careful jurist whose opinions never quite overcame a writing style one critic called "rodomontade." He possessed an almost photographic memory for citations and his 700 opinions over 27 years on the Court are filled with so many precedents that they represent "models of what judicial opinions ought not to be." Nevertheless, he became an almost beloved part of the Washington scene even though, like Chief Justice Fuller, he disdained its social life. Despite his sizable girth, he became a familiar figure walking around District parks.

When Melville Fuller died in July, 1910, President William Howard Taft surprised the nation by nominating the sixty-six year old White as chief justice. Taft had filled previous vacancies with younger men, but later told President Warren Harding that White had agreed that he "was holding the office for me, and that he would give it back to me in a Republican Administration." Whatever the truth of that assertion, even in 1910 some suspected Taft was indeed preparing his own path to the Court. In any event, it was White who in December, 1910, became the ninth chief justice of the United States.

For the next eleven years, White led a Court that maintained the conservative approach of Chief Justice Fuller, yet was more interesting and innovative than either that Court or the Taft bench that succeeded his tenure. In 1911, White orchestrated the Court's decisions in the *Standard Oil* and *American Tobacco* litigation, and pronounced that the Sherman Anti-Trust Act of 1890 outlawed only "unreasonable" combinations in restraint of trade. The oil monopoly qualified as unreasonable and so could be broken up by the federal government, while the tobacco industry did not. White's "rule of reason" became the standard of judgment for a generation, even though the definition of "unreasonable" varied widely over the course of many decisions. His Court considered the use of federal police power quite legitimate, and so upheld the Pure Food and Drug Act, a revised employers' liability law, the White Slavery Act, and the ICC's power to set intrastate railroad rates. It was obvious that White's conservativism was capable of permitting a great deal of government activity on behalf of the public interest and, during his tenure, Justice Oliver Wendell Holmes, Jr., whose dissents had punctuated the Fuller years, often joined his vote to the new majority. In 1916, White promulgated perhaps his most significant decision when he wrote the majority opinion upholding the Adamson Act permitting government control of both wages and hours in the railroad industry during the wartime emergency. The thrust of his Court was to soften judicial opposition to government action on behalf of the general population, yet also to protect individuals against a too aggressive central authority. In the *Weeks* decision of 1914, for example, White's unanimous Court declared that evidence improperly obtained by government agents could not be used against a defendant in federal proceedings.

As the leader of the Court, White unceasingly sought to eliminate procedural roadblocks to action. Always a hard worker, he tried to argue his brethren into a compromise opinion rather than totally ignore an issue. He won a reputation for being kind to lawyers appearing before the bench, yet demanded that they reduce argument time to one and a half hours. Since 1873, the Court had convened the second week of October, but White changed this to the first Monday in October, a practice the modern Court still honors. His Court ran efficiently and, if he did not dominate it in the fashion of a Marshall or a Taney, his was a benign presence. When World War I finally drew the United States into combat, the White Court rallied to the colors also and its *Selective Draft Law* (1918) and *Schenck* decisions (1919) unanimously upheld the powers of the government to effectively fight a global war.

When the Republicans elected Warren Harding as president in 1920, Chief Justice White was already past seventy-five. His longevity was known to irritate former President Taft, a feeling intensified when White rejected his pension and opted to remain on the bench. His eyesight was deteriorating because of cataracts, and his formidable memory was now failing, but he refused all suggestions that he resign. Fate, however, stepped in. After a six day illness, this relatively unknown, but quietly effective chief justice, died on May 19, 1921, after having served the Court and nation for twenty-seven years.

WILLIAM HOWARD TAFT
September 15, 1857 - March 8, 1930
Chief Justice: June 30, 1921 - February 3, 1930

Few individuals in American history have served the Republic in as many capacities as William Howard Taft. Not since the age of the Founding Fathers had a man so successfully blended the arts of the politician with the expertise of the public servant. Taft remains the only man in our history to lead both the executive and judicial branches of the government; he considered appointment to the Court the crowning achievement of his long career. He utilized the position of chief justice in a more political way than any of his predecessors, acting in a fashion that modern analysts of the bench would deem improper. Despite his critics, however, Taft never doubted either his motives or his rectitude. During the decade he led the Court, he built a federal judiciary which mirrored his own political conservatism and enjoyed national prestige. Under him, the Court became "a bulwark to enforce the guarantee that no man shall be deprived of his property without due process of law." During the decade that historians call the "Roaring Twenties," Taft embodied conservative principles. Although he was never a reactionary, Taft's instincts led him to defend the *status quo*, *laissez faire*, verities of a booming age of enterprise. During his tenure, a conservative Court majority invalidated more legislation than during the fifty years preceding his appointment to America's highest court.

Taft was born in Cincinnati on September 15, 1857, and shared the solid value system of middle America. Public service was a duty of citizenship, and his grandfather, father, and elder brother all built successful political careers, which Taft later eclipsed. After attending a public high school, Taft graduated as the salutatorian of the Yale class of 1878, and then entered Cincinnati Law School. He received his law degree in 1880, passed the bar, and began his long career in Republican politics. He served successively as Hamilton County's assistant prosecutor, its solicitor, and then as an Ohio Superior Court judge. His marriage in 1886 to Helen Herren proved a happy one that produced three children. He soon advanced to the position of U.S. Solicitor General, and won fifteen of his eighteen cases before the Supreme Court before himself becoming a federal circuit court judge. In 1900, President William McKinley named Taft Chairman of the Philippine Commission, whose task was to facilitate the transition of the islands from military to civilian rule; he subsequently served as Governor of the territory. Amazingly, in the face of virtually constant movement on behalf of the nation, his marriage thrived. It is interesting to note that Taft's son and grandson served in the Senate of the United States, where they continued the family tradition of public service.

In 1904, Taft came to Washington as secretary of war and began his career in national politics. He became one of President Theodore Roosevelt's closest advisors, oversaw the start of the Panama Canal project, and virtually had the presidency bestowed upon him when Roosevelt retired from the White House in 1908. Even at that time, however, many suspected that Taft would have preferred a Supreme Court appointment because his truest vocation was the law and he disdained the intrigues of Washington politics. His presidency proved competent and featured a continuation of high tariff economic policies, trust busting, creation of a postal savings system, and the ratification of the income tax amendment. President Taft also named six justices to the Supreme Court in only four years, including an aging Edward D. White as chief justice. But Taft's serenity was destroyed by his differences with Theodore Roosevelt over policy and programs; their feud ultimately led to the Bull Moose insurrection of 1912 that splintered the Republican Party and led to the election of Woodrow Wilson as president. After March, 1913, Taft taught constitutional law at Yale, served a term as president of the American Bar Association, and headed the League to Enforce Peace (1915). He frequently wrote on public affairs and, in 1916, joined an abortive Republican effort to defeat the nomination of Louis Brandeis, "a Jew and a Democrat," to the Supreme Court. Despite his scorn for the president's choice, Taft discreetly let Wilson understand that he himself would be available for appointment to the high court. He demonstrated his willingness to serve a Democratic president by accepting the joint chairmanship of the National War Labor Board, and actively touring on behalf of the League of Nations.

When Chief Justice White died, it seemed inevitable that President Warren Harding would select Taft to replace him. The nomination was made on June 30, 1921, and confirmed by the Senate on the same day with only four dissenting votes. Taft, after dreaming of it for years, finally had attained his desire to lead the Supreme Court. But it was a Court divided between ideological blocs, with dissents appearing in 25% of all opinions. Taft worked hard to reduce tension among the justices, and there were only about 200 further dissents in the next decade. The new chief ordered that oral argument before the Court be reduced to an hour, and then turned toward improving procedures in the national judicial system. Administration, not law, became Taft's primary concern, and many believe that he conceded the intellectual leadership of the Court to Justice Willis Van Devanter as he concentrated his efforts on judicial efficiency. In 1922, Taft won Congressional approval for the creation of a Judicial Conference of Senior Circuit Judges chaired by the chief justice, a body which, in time, did accomplish a considerable modernization of the system. Then, in February, 1925, his lobbying was vital in winning acceptance for the Judge's Bill, a measure that permitted the Supreme Court far more discretion in deciding which cases it would accept for review; he also persuaded Congress to authorize construction of a new home for the Supreme Court. As a result of Taft's initiatives, the Court had become current with its docket by 1930. Since Taft, all chief justices have had far greater responsibility for managing the judicial system than most Americans realize, although it is a role that several chiefs have not relished.

But if Taft won praise as an administrator, the Court he led was weak and predictable. This chief was overtly political, and constantly advised Republican presidents on policy matters and vacancies throughout the judicial system. His concern was not that only Republicans be appointed, but rather men who shared his conservative viewpoint. Taft's own judicial decisions normally reflected the bedrock principles on which his career had been based. His first major opinion in 1921 argued that the state of Arizona could not forbid issuance of injunctions against picketing. As a conservative, Taft evidenced distaste for legislation that had social goals, and *Bailey v. Drexel Furniture* (1922) voided a federal child labor law because it improperly used taxing power to achieve societal ends. He was not totally consistent, however, since, in 1923, he dissented when the Court majority found a minimum wage law to be unconstitutional in *Adkins*. He understood that low paid employees were "peculiarly subject to the . . . harsh and greedy employer," but he was unable or unwilling to bring the Court over to that humane position. The majority he had partially named and consistently lobbied for was more conservative than its creator. But Taft's Court did decide *Gitlow v. New York*, the first of a long series of rulings which, using the Fourteenth Amendment, applied the Bill of Rights to states. Finally, in ex-President Taft's most significant decision, *Myers v. United States* in 1926, he sustained a president's right to remove executive officials without Congressional approval, a grant of power to the executive recognizing its primacy over the legislative branch. He also upheld the government's right to tap the phones of bootleggers; his decision in *Olmsted* in 1928 held "there was no searching. There was no seizure. The evidence was secured by the sense of hearing" and so the Fourteenth Amendment was not violated.

Taft remains the only American ever to serve both as president and chief justice. Yet the decade he spent on the Court as a legal reformer and titular head of the American judicial system was probably the most satisfying time of his life. He saw his ideas of judicial efficiency implemented, and believed that his adherence to principle had made America a safer society, one free from the radicalism that could threaten its moral and economic foundations. Such an uncomplicated vision of American life would not have been possible in the 1930s, but Taft was never asked to cope with the effects of the Great Depression. He was worn out by a lifetime of service to the nation, and from the cumulative strain of carrying excess weight. His increasing feebleness due to heart disease led him to resign from the Court on February 3, 1930. Less than five weeks later, on March 8th, Taft died in Washington and was accorded the honor of an Arlington Cemetery burial. Few men had so long and so devotedly served their nation.

CHARLES EVANS HUGHES

April 11, 1862 - August 17, 1948

Chief Justice: February 13, 1930 - July 1, 1941

Charles Evans Hughes was twice appointed a member of the Supreme Court, a unique achievement in American legal history. During his stint as an associate justice (1910-1916), he had provocatively written that the United States is "under a Constitution, but the Constitution is what the judges say it is." The remark was witty and wise, as befitted a man who fashioned one of the great careers in twentieth century law. Yet Hughes' subsequent appointment as chief justice proved the truth of the sentence as well, since he took charge of an almost reactionary Court and presided over its transformation into one that endorsed the social experimentation of the New Deal. Hughes' role in this evolution is much discussed by scholars – one of his brethren likened Hughes in conference to "Toscanini lead[ing] an orchestra" – but exactly how the chief justice accomplished this sea change in legal attitudes remains something of a marvel. Some analysts consider Hughes the premier chief of the century, while others find him a political chameleon, but all agree his impact on the Court and his age was significant. Some go so far as to assert that Hughes was responsible for maintaining the independence of the third branch of government against executive assault.

Hughes was the only child of an abolitionist minister who lived in Glens Falls, New York. He was born during the Civil War, on April 11, 1862, and was raised in a home filled with moral fervor and Baptist rectitude. His parents relocated to New York City when their boy was eight, and privately tutored him in preparation for a ministerial career. He entered Madison College (Colgate) at the age of fourteen, transferred to Brown College in 1878, and graduated Phi Beta Kappa at the age of nineteen. Deciding to become a lawyer rather than a minister, he taught Greek, Latin, and mathematics at a rural school in order to raise money for law school tuition. The young man's private reading of law facilitated his entrance to Columbia Law School, and he graduated after only two years with highest honors; he got 99 on his bar exam in 1884. For the next twenty years, Hughes juggled the careers of corporate attorney and full Professor of Law at Cornell University, while attaining a reputation as one of Manhattan's finest lawyers. In New York, Justice Benjamin Cardozo made it a rule to wait a day before deciding any point that Hughes argued, while Judge Learned Hand consistently cautioned himself to believe that Hughes "isn't necessarily right." He married Antoinette Carter on December 5, 1888, and they had three children during their almost idyllic life together.

In 1905, Hughes entered public service for the first time. He was named counsel to the Stevens Gas Commission, which discovered systematic overcharging of utility customers in New York State; his year on the Armstrong Insurance Commission uncovered fraud and racketeering in the insurance industry. Hughes' investigatory labors made him a national figure and, with the endorsement of President Theodore Roosevelt, Empire State Republicans made him their gubernatorial candidate; the neophyte politician became the only party candidate to win statewide election in 1906. In 1907, the Hughes' became the parents of the first child ever born in Albany's Executive Mansion. Hughes won an even larger victory two years later and, in 1910, President Taft asked him to accept nomination to the Supreme Court. The reluctant governor agreed: "I had no right to refuse. A refusal on the ground that . . . I might be a candidate for the Presidency . . . would have been absurd." In the Senate, not a single vote was cast against his nomination and, for the six years following May, 1910, he built a generally liberal voting record on White's Court. He wrote opinions that made it illegal for employers to compel their employees to work off debts and upheld a California maximum hour law; he generally supported a broad view of Congress' right to regulate trade and commerce.

Hughes' reputation as a humane nationalist grew rapidly and, in the summer of 1916, he was nominated for president by both the Republican and the Progressive Parties. He resigned from the Court on June 10th, and ran a strong campaign against Woodrow Wilson; the change of only 4,800 votes in California would have made Hughes president. Afterward, he returned to the practice of law as senior partner of a New York firm and as an advisor to corporate America. Personal reasons led him to rebuff presidential booms in both 1920 and 1928, but he did serve as Secretary of State from 1921 to 1925; he was considered the dominant figure at the Washington Disarmament Conference (1921). In an age of isolationism, Hughes believed in an international role for America and, after his retirement from government, became United States representative at the International Court of Arbitration and the Permanent Court of International Justice (1926-1930). The Bronx County Bar Association honored him in 1929 as "the perfect citizen."

On February 3, 1930, almost twenty years after Hughes' first nomination to the Supreme Court, President Herbert Hoover submitted his name to the Senate as chief justice. Despite his prominence, his Jovian appearance, and his erudition – Hughes had actually written a history of the Supreme Court – many Senators believed the nominee was too closely identified with "powerful combinations in the political and financial worlds." The Crash of October, 1929, was fresh in the minds of many who opposed this corporate lawyer's ascent to the high bench, but, after ten days of contentious debate, the nomination was approved by a vote of

52-26. For the next eleven years, Hughes piloted the Court through shoals as America drifted through the horrors of the Depression. He brought to his chief's position the advantages of a photographic memory, an imposing judicial presence, a commitment to civil liberties, and the skills of a politician. Moreover, according to Justice Jackson, Hughes always "looked like God and talked like God." During the spring of 1931, his Court decided two major free speech cases, *Stromberg v. California* and *Near v. Minnesota*, with the chief justice's opinion broadening First Amendment rights against state infringement; these were two of the most important of some 350 opinions he wrote as chief. During his tenure, Hughes always insisted that justices consider fully the constitutional implications of all appeals to the Court. His concern for the rights of the indigent petitioner made him, in the words of Justice Felix Frankfurter, the "leader of the legal aid movement." Hughes himself read all briefs and could not understand why his brethren sometimes had trouble deciding on their deposition. Harlen Stone considered Hughes a virtual "drill sergeant" who demanded rapid disposition of appeals in order to keep the Court up to date. Indeed, Hughes' reputation for efficiency was such that one lawyer remembered the chief ordering him to end oral argument in the middle of the word "if." Whether by such rigor or simply by hard work, the Hughes Court was always current with its docket.

If Hughes' attitude toward the expansion of the Bill of Rights was consistent, his position regarding economic regulation was ambiguous. As the ravages of the Great Depression became ever more apparent, the election of the Democrats in 1932 signalled a more innovative approach to economic legislation than conservative jurists wished to contemplate. The Court was filled with Republican appointees, and Hughes had long been identified with a corporate America now struggling under new circumstances. More than his conservative brethren, however, Hughes understood that federal power must expand to cope with the problems of modern economics. His opinions on New Deal legislation, therefore, seem somewhat inconsistent unless they are read as seeking a new middle ground for the Court, a shifting of judicial approach to make the law more receptive to the actions of the legislative and executive branches. When the Court was united Hughes wrote decisions, such as *Schechter* in 1935, which invalidated poorly drawn New Deal legislation. In the *Butler* decision of 1936, he seemed to shift his vote in order to have the Court appear more united that it actually was. In still other cases, the chief justice tried to create a more liberal majority against the reactionary attitudes of several justices by making use of his power to name the writer of a decision. Always, he was ready to defend his bench against charges it was out of tune with economic reality, a "horse and buggy" Court in a modern age.

It is unnecessary here to recount the duel between President Franklin D. Roosevelt and the Hughes Court, but there is little doubt that FDR's "Court Packing" plan of 1937 was defeated in large part because of the political astuteness of the chief justice. Even before Roosevelt had an opportunity to name Democratic members to the Court, Hughes had created, and was acting as the leader of, a narrow, but real, Court majority which found New Deal legislation acceptable. The internal dynamics of the "switch in time that saved nine" is the subject of many books, but analysts agree that Chief Justice Hughes helped to create that new consensus. The altered Court attitude toward the initiatives of Roosevelt's New Deal provided Hughes with the arguments that repulsed the executive's attempt to expand, i.e. "pack," the Supreme Court.

If the Constitution is "what the judges say it is," then Hughes' reign as chief illuminates the process whereby that document is constantly reinterpreted to suit the needs of a new age. Hughes moved the Court away from mindless rejection of socially innovative legislation to a position that enabled it to recapture public support. He proved himself not only an adept manager of the third branch, but also a masterly politician capable of facing down the greatest president of our century. If Hughes sometimes kept the honor of writing major decisions for himself, as he did in many critical cases from 1935 to 1941, that is perhaps the special prerogative due a great leader of the Court. Better than any justice since Marshall, he made the commerce clause fit the needs of a growing nation and his court's expansive view of Congressional power dominated American jurisprudence for 60 years. Hughes had since his youth been athletically inclined, he climbed mountains in the 1890s and even as chief justice daily walked around the Capitol, but now time began to take its inevitable toll. On June 2, 1941, he wrote President Roosevelt regarding his wish to retire due to "considerations of health and age." The request was naturally honored and, the next year, the American Bar Association awarded the retired chief its highest honor for "conspicuous service" to American jurisprudence. On August 17, 1948, the eighty-six year old Hughes died while vacationing on Cape Cod. He was buried from Riverside Church and laid to rest in Woodlawn Cemetery, The Bronx. It was the end of an era in American law.

HARLAN FISKE STONE
October 11, 1872 - April 22, 1946
Chief Justice: June 27, 1941 - April 22, 1946

W hen Chief Justice Hughes decided to retire in 1941, he confronted President Roosevelt with a delicate political problem as well as the opportunity to firmly establish a more liberal Supreme Court. Since the defeat of the "Court Packing" scheme in 1937, death and retirement had enabled Roosevelt to name five associate justices in less than three years, and the new line up had already proven itself more favorable to social and economic legislation by the federal government. But the many critics of the administration condemned what they termed partisanship in Roosevelt's judicial nominations. The president was anxious not to affront any senator, since it appeared increasingly likely that the war in Europe might soon extend itself to the United States. It was Hughes who suggested that Roosevelt might demonstrate a national vision by reaching into the Court and moving a nominal Republican justice to the chief's seat. The elevation of Edward D. White served as a precedent for such a shift and it would permit Roosevelt to select two associates, since Justice James McReynolds also intended to resign. The president could act in a bipartisan manner yet, at the same time, consolidate the new liberal majority on the Court. Roosevelt was easily convinced and accepted Hughes' suggestion that he nominate Harlan Fiske Stone to the center chair. Senate confirmation made Stone the first and only man in American history to fill every seat on the Court, from junior associate to chief justice.

Stone was born in Chesterfield, New Hampshire, on October 11, 1872 into a family that traced its Puritan roots back to 1635. He was raised on a farm, yet went on to graduate Phi Beta Kappa from Amherst College, where he was class president and a varsity football player. After briefly teaching science in high school, "Slug" Stone enrolled at Columbia Law School and graduated with honors in 1898. He won admission to the New York bar the next year, and married Agnes Harvey in September; they had two sons. Stone worked as a corporate attorney for Sullivan and Cromwell until 1903, when he joined the faculty of Columbia Law School. Although he always maintained a small private practice, Stone remained at that school for the next twenty years. He served as dean for many years and engaged in a celebrated feud with Nicolas M. Butler, president of the university. On April 1, 1924, Stone was named Attorney General of the United States with the task of restoring the prestige of the Justice Department after the Harding administration scandals. He was responsible for the selection of J. Edgar Hoover to lead the FBI, and insisted that the anti-trust division be expanded. After less than a year, a vacancy on the Court occurred, and President Calvin Coolidge named his fellow Amherst alumnus to the position. Stone's reputation was impeccable, but some Senators opposed him because of his Wall Street background; he became the first nominee to undergo systematic questioning by the Senate Judiciary Committee before his confirmation on February 5, 1925.

When Stone joined the Court, it was assumed that he would enter the conservative bloc because he had demonstrated a faith in *laissez faire* economics and actually been once retained as J.P. Morgan's lawyer. Yet, within a few years, he established himself as a justice who saw the Constitution as an evolving document that permitted social reform. He became a frequent dissenter on the Taft Court and often joined with Justices Holmes and Brandeis to oppose the static vision of the majority. Stone was a recognized member of Herbert Hoover's "medicine ball" cabinet, but refused to lead the president's Law Enforcement Commission because it would conflict with his duties as a justice. Reportedly, Stone offered to resign in 1930 so that Hoover might name Benjamin Cardozo, a man Stone considered the greatest appellate judge in America, to the Court, but the president declined to permit this. Taft, already entering his last illness, let it be known that he opposed the elevation of Stone to the chief's seat; he "is not a leader and would have a great deal of trouble massing the Court." When Hughes was selected, a leak before the president's press conference still asserted that the position would go to Stone, to the mortification of both men. During the Depression years, Stone proved generally sympathetic to Roosevelt's legislative program and was one of only three justices who found the Agricultural Adjustment Act to be constitutional. His bitter dissent affirming that the Supreme Court is not "the only agency of government that must be assumed to have the capacity to govern," was remembered by Roosevelt when he contemplated naming Stone the chief justice. Political advantage, as well as the support of the bar, the press, and the public, all were reflected in the ringing voice vote of the Senate that confirmed the nomination on June 27, 1941.

Despite high expectations, the five years that Stone led the Supreme Court were not happy ones. Unlike both his immediate predecessors, he had little interest in administering or managing the larger judicial system. Moreover, he never achieved firm control of the liberal Court he headed. Demonstrating a professor's need to analyze cases from every angle, Stone had long chaffed under the rapid fire conference style of Hughes. As chief, he went to the opposite extreme and permitted conferences to ramble on so long that Justice William O. Douglas, who had studied law with Stone at Columbia, considered them "continuous." Stone's Court was perhaps the most brilliant of the century, but his failure to exert full leadership permitted the associate justices so much latitude that each began to operate independently. The practice of multiple concurring opinions, so remarked upon today, first surfaced as a phenomenon of the Stone Court. As opinions diverged, personal animosity emerged as a force on the Court; Stone had the unhappy duty of mediating the bitter personal clashes between Justices Jackson and Black, and was himself occasionally guilty of harsh comments about his brethren. Stone had great talents as a judge but his tenure as chief illuminated the different skills necessary to preside over the Court rather than merely write decisions. Perhaps Roosevelt sensed the disarray, for he offered Stone the post of "rubber czar" during the war, but the chief justice declined that appointment on the same grounds that he had earlier used with Hoover.

Whatever Stone's failings, his Court continued to look with favor on the expansion of federal power. During his first year as chief, ten precedents were overturned generally in the direction of enhancing government authority in regard to labor relations, commerce, and spending power. Stone had established his own attitude favoring such economic regulation as early as 1938, but he also maintained that the presumption in favor of federal authority did not extend to Bill of Rights freedoms. He was consistent in his support of civil liberties, and when his Court upheld Pennsylvania's compulsory flag salute law, Stone was the only dissenter. In other rights decisions, his Court overturned the white primary, forbade Jim Crowism on interstate bus lines, and prohibited "restrictive covenants" in housing. But liberalism could not consistently survive the pressures of war, and Stone was with the majority in both *Hirabyashi* (1943) and *Korematsu* (1944) which upheld government actions against Japanese-Americans. Stone's dedication to the Court and his conception of liberty continued to the day he died. On April 22, 1946, while reading his dissent in a naturalization case, he was stricken by a massive cerebral hemorrhage and died at the age of 74.

FREDERICK MOORE VINSON
January 22, 1890 - September 8, 1953
Chief Justice: June 20, 1946 - September 8, 1953

The sudden death of Chief Justice Stone provided Harry S Truman with an opportunity every president longs for, the chance to name a leader of the Supreme Court. Truman wished to appoint a justice who would understand that strong executive authority was necessary because the United States faced the dangers of a Cold War with the Soviet Union. But unlike President Roosevelt, Truman felt no need to placate the Republican Party with his selection. Nevertheless, it took him six weeks to decide on an old friend, Fred M. Vinson, who was so staunch a New Dealer that he had supported the "Court Packing" plan of 1937. Vinson also had judicial experience and political expertise, and the president calculated that the latter might be essential because Justice Robert Jackson, who wanted to be chief, had publicly criticized one of his brethren. Personality clashes had become so common that analysts likened Court dynamics to putting "nine scorpions in a bottle." But Truman believed that Vinson had the ability to accommodate opposing views and forwarded the nomination to the Senate on June 6, 1946. After only two weeks of perfunctory hearings, the Senate endorsed Vinson by a voice vote and consented to his appointment as the thirteenth Chief Justice of the United States.

Fred Vinson was born on January 22, 1890, in the small hamlet of Louisa, Kentucky. The family was poor; his father ran the county jail, and the young boy attended the local school. He worked his way through Center College, and then obtained a law degree from that institution in 1911. He was only twenty-one when he passed the Kentucky bar exam, and spent the next two decades in active practice; his investments in local mills and banks secured financial status for his family. Vinson first entered Democratic politics as Ashland City Attorney, served afterwards as Commonwealth Attorney, and then won a House seat from Kentucky's 9th Congressional District. Shortly before his election, he married Roberta Dixson, with whom he had two sons. With the exception of one term, he served in the House from 1924 to 1938, and became an influential member of the Ways and Means Committee. He developed New Deal tax programs and worked to protect Kentucky's coal interests. In 1938, when President Roosevelt offered Vinson an appointment to the Circuit Court of Appeals of the District of Columbia, he resigned his seat and donned a black robe. But his tax knowledge and administrative skills were needed during the war, and, after 1943, he successively served in the Office of Economic Stabilization, as Federal Loan Administrator, and as Director of War Mobilization and Reconversion. Vinson's friendship with Truman dated back to the 1930s and, when the new president asked him to join his cabinet in 1945, the "assistant President" willingly made the switch.

Secretary of the Treasury Vinson coordinated the final war bond drives and recommended higher taxes to fund the transition to a peacetime economy. He believed that the changed world situation demanded stronger federal authority to meet domestic and foreign policy challenges, and was a trusted advisor as Truman struggled to adapt the nation to the postwar environment. His intellectual compatibility with Truman made him an obvious choice as chief justice once the post became available.

The president believed that Vinson's political skills and patient nature could restore decorum to a factionalized Court. If he could influence its psychology towards accepting the decisions of the legislative and executive branches of government, that would be an added bonus. Vinson did tend to trust the will of the representatives of the people, and normally argued that the Court ought to accept only cases that were extremely important or raised constitutional issues. As a result of this approach, the case load of the Supreme Court fell drastically during Vinson's tenure; only once did it even handle a hundred cases, against Hughes' average of 200 decisions yearly. The diplomatically minded chief split opinion writing almost equally among all justices and obtained for each of them a second law clerk. An "executive officer," named to help the chief justice administer the judicial system, eased the paperwork burden that had helped crush Stone. Some analysts see Vinson's as a "lazy" Court because of these changes, but, at the very least, a semblance of collegiality was restored and the work pressures eased. Vinson himself conceded that he was no legal scholar and hardly seemed to mind that he wrote relatively few opinions. But he always remained available to advise the president either by phone or on the long fishing weekends they shared at Key West.

Vinson maintained his friendship with the president to an inordinate, even improper, degree and he also strove to provide Truman with an understanding Supreme Court. Both men believed that a powerful federal government responsive to the will of the majority was best for America, and the rise of a communist enemy made this goal seem even more imperative. Vinson thus led a Cold War Court, one that generally believed the government had to protect itself from domestic and foreign enemies, even if civil liberties might suffer. The chief justice's majority opinion in the 1950 case of *American Communications Association v. Douds* held that labor union officials could be required to swear they were not communists. It even hinted that Congress had the right to interfere with free speech. Vinson again spoke for the Court in *Dennis v. United States* when it upheld convictions of communists under the Smith Act. Some critics of the Court denounced these decisions as abridgments of the

First Amendment, but Vinson saw them as supportive of federal initiatives to meet the challenge of communism. His Court let the Rosenbergs die in 1953, after Chief Justice Vinson convened a special session to overturn a stay granted by Justice Douglas. The rigor of this Court applied to aliens as well, since decisions approving deportations and detention without bail were issued. The Court also upheld federal power against the states in regard to ownership of coastal oil rights and in voiding "fair trade" laws. In general, Vinson believed that government authority to protect the nation was paramount, and that individual liberties had to yield in any confrontation. When the Court refused to uphold President Truman's authority to seize the nation's steel mills, Vinson was part of the minority favoring executive power.

But in regard to the constitutional rights of Black Americans, the Vinson Court did foreshadow future events. Vinson spoke for a unanimous Court in the *Sweatt* and *McLaurin* decisions of 1950 which guaranteed Black access to higher education and signalled the erosion of the "separate but equal" doctrine in place since 1896. Some analysts question Vinson's personal commitment to total desegregation, since he reportedly did not favor integrated educational facilities, but there is no doubt that decisions by his Court did pave the way for the subsequent civil rights revolution initiated by the Warren Court. President Truman never ceased to have faith in his appointee, however, and even hoped that the Democrats might nominate Vinson for the presidency in 1952. Vinson quickly put an end to that trial balloon and remained on the Court until he suffered a heart attack and died, September 8, 1953.

EARL WARREN
March 19, 1891 - July 9, 1974
Chief Justice: March 1, 1954 - June 23, 1969

In an address at New York's Jewish Theological Seminary in 1962, Chief Justice Earl Warren tried to explain his views of law and the Constitution, attitudes which had made him the twentieth century's most controversial and vilified leader of the Supreme Court. He argued that there is a "Law beyond the Law," an ethical standard of conduct that good men ought to follow, and that it was the task of a United States judge to "discern the right in the midst of great confusion and to pursue it." The Founding Fathers held this moral vision of life and wrote a Constitution which drew distinctions between right and wrong, freedom and intolerance, so that the United States might always have the ability to be a just society. The Bill of Rights, Warren wrote elsewhere, codified the American sense of justice in defense of "the natural rights of men" and was intended to guarantee the equality, privacy, and dignity of all men before the law. In our national history, the Bill of Rights constantly evolved as judges articulated the meaning of their rights for each new generation of Americans. But the goal of equality remained steady. Warren's dynamic view of the judge's role in this process led President Dwight Eisenhower to declare that his appointment to the Court was "the biggest damn-fool mistake I ever made." Yet that same moral vision permits many scholars to label Warren the greatest chief justice since Marshall. Like his illustrious predecessor, Warren had a revolutionary impact on the history of his nation.

Earl Warren was born in Los Angeles on March 19, 1891, the son of Norwegian immigrants who, soon after, settled in California's San Joaquin Valley. His father was a railroad mechanic, and the young man worked his way through both college and law school at the University of California. He was admitted to the California bar in 1914 and engaged in private practice until he entered the army as a first lieutenant during World War I. After completing his military obligation, Warren was named deputy city attorney of Oakland in 1919. That appointment began 50 continuous years of public service which would take him from municipal office to leadership of the "Marble Temple" of the Supreme Court. On October 25, 1925, he married Nina Meyers, and the couple had six children. Warren first won fame as a district attorney tough on organized crime in Alameda County, and his investigations of municipal corruption sent several incumbent politicians to prison. In 1938, the year his father was murdered in an unsolved crime, Warren was elected attorney general of California with the endorsement of all state parties. Now a proven vote getter, he won the first of three consecutive terms as California's governor in 1942 by defeating the Democratic incumbent. During World War II, he embodied conservative attitudes, denouncing communists and supporting relocation of

Japanese-Americans into detention centers. But after 1945, Warren steadily moved to endorse more progressive policies; he proposed a radical program of prepaid medical care, rejected loyalty oaths for employment, and obtained legislation enacting pension and welfare reforms. In the elections of 1946 and 1950, he was the gubernatorial choice of both the Republican and Democratic parties and won a national reputation for his mastery of state politics. Warren did consider himself a Republican, however, and was the losing vice presidential candidate of that party in 1948. At the convention of 1952, he used California's strength to secure the nomination for Eisenhower, and put the new president in his debt. When Chief Justice Vinson died in 1953, Ike repaid the debt by sending Warren's nomination to the Senate, which approved it by a voice vote on March 1, 1954.

The year 1954 saw the Supreme Court issue only sixty-four decisions, but the term was marked by one great case, the voiding of legal public school segregation in *Brown v. Board of Education of Topeka*. Warren spoke for the Court as it put an end to the "separate but equal" doctrine, and his managerial skill in obtaining a unanimous verdict from a previously divided court in a matter of such importance was hailed as a prime example of judicial statesmanship. Despite the immediate outcry from the Deep South against "judicial legislation," the Court ordered in 1955 that desegregation proceed with "all deliberate speed." Warren told the nation that "the vitality of these court principles cannot be allowed to yield simply because of disagreement." A decent and reasonable man, Warren believed that his bench could lead all fair-minded Americans to endorse that goal. Under Warren, the Supreme Court became the moral conscience of the nation and the most dynamic initiator of social change in the American government. He was also the first chief to align the Court with modern technology when he ordered the tape recording of oral arguments during the 1955 term.

Before he became chief justice, Warren had no judicial experience; yet, his fifteen year tenure on the Court made a revolution in constitutional law and changed the lives of millions of Americans. There are still critics who fault the sociological and psychological reasoning of the *Brown* decision, but the Court's ruling inspired the subsequent civil rights movement that has transformed the lives of Black Americans. Moreover, the Court insisted that the nation follow its lead in fulfilling the promise of equality. When Little Rock, Arkansas, and Governor Orval Faubus attempted to delay desegregation of schools in 1958, Warren convened a special session of the Court and had every justice sign the ruling that ordered compliance. Deciding *Baker v. Carr* in 1962, the Court entered the "political thicket" of representation to rule that maldistribution of voter population in legislative districts could be rectified by federal courts. Then Warren's *Reynold v. Sims* ruling in 1964 applied the "one person, one vote" rule to all houses of state legislatures.

Warren's Court applied the guarantees of the Bill of Rights to the states as well as the federal government. Whether discovering the existence of a right to privacy in *Griswold* in 1965 or mandating that defense attorneys be supplied to indigent criminals (*Gideon*, 1963), the Warren Court insisted that all persons are entitled to due process of law and that government on every level must respect individual rights. Unlike Vinson, who instinctively favored federal authority, Warren sought to offer the full protection of the Constitution to each individual regardless of his position in society. His Court understood that such guarantees were meaningless unless they were actually extended to witnesses, suspects, and defendants in criminal procedures. In a series of controversial decisions, *Mapp* (1961), *Escobedo* (1964), and *Miranda* (1966), the Warren Court forced basic reforms in police procedure. He and his brethren had no hesitancy in forcing the other two branches to adhere to constitutional behavior; for example, the *Powell* decision of 1969 ordered the House of Representatives to abide by the words of the Constitution when seating its membership. The justices continued to enhance the meaning of the Bill of Rights; the First Amendment's freedom of the press guarantee was extended greatly by their unanimous decision in the case of *New York Times v. Sullivan* in 1964. In tumultuous times, Warren and his brethren made a revolution in the ways American society worked. Liberals praised their efforts, while conservative criticism ran the gamut from those who found the Court's reasoning faulty to zealots who simply wanted to "impeach Earl Warren."

Warren, a bearish, good-natured and kindly man, accepted criticism as part of his job. He ran a generally happy Court and fully restored its lost sense of collegiality, though a few commentators believe that the multiplicity of opinion writing that bedevils the current Court increased during his tenure. The Constitution does not specify that a member of the Supreme Court must be a lawyer, but is nonetheless amazing to discover that not until 1957 did all sitting members of the Court simultaneously hold law degrees; an attorney's inevitable desire to make an independent argument has been on the rise ever since. Warren knew he was no legal scholar and, initially, was unfamiliar with Court procedure; yet, his compelling ethical view of the Constitution made him the most influential chief justice of this century. One of his misjudgments, however, was accepting leadership of the Commission which investigated the assassination of John F. Kennedy. Warren had respected Kennedy and occasionally advised him on judicial appointments. He felt a citizen's obligation to help President Lyndon Johnson put an end to the rumors of conspiracy that surfaced after Kennedy's death. The Warren Commission report of September, 1964, was voluminous and thorough, but failed to end those rumors. Perhaps the entire episode proved that chief justices ought always to remain on the bench. In 1968, after half a century of public service and fifteen years on the high court, Warren believed he deserved retirement and informed President Johnson of his intention to resign once a successor had won approval. The president's choice to succeed the "Super Chief" was Justice Abe Fortas, but the nomination ran into election year complications because of charges of excessive teaching fees and "cronyism." The nomination was therefore withdrawn by President Johnson. When the national election resulted in a change of government, it became the duty of a rather disillusioned Warren to swear in his successor. On June 23, 1969, he administered the oath to Warren Burger, although he privately believed the fifteenth chief justice would prove to be a "doctrinaire law-and-order judge" more concerned with upholding convictions than with broadening Constitutional principles. During his later years, it was reported that Warren delighted in reading volumes that chronicled the Watergate scandal. After enjoying five years of the retirement he had sought, a heart attack ended Warren's life on July 9, 1974. He was buried with high national honors in Arlington Cemetery.

WARREN EARL BURGER
September 17, 1907 – June 25, 1995
Chief Justice: June 9, 1969 - June 17, 1986

A major campaign theme of Richard Nixon's successful race for the presidency in 1968 was his promise to name "strict constructionists" to the Supreme Court. Rarely in our history had the Court been so politically controversial, for many conservatives believed it had usurped the legislative powers of Congress and was imposing the liberal viewpoint of unelected judges on the American people. The Court was berated as being opposed to "law and order" and overly concerned with the rights of criminals rather than sympathetic to their victims. It was attacked as favoring pornography, being anti-religious, and of ignoring the rights of the white majority in its concern for racial equality. Chief Justice Warren symbolized all these perverse trends, and the new president was elated with his immediate opportunity to change the Court's leadership. Great reforms were expected after the appointment of Warren Burger, but his career as chief justice illustrates how very difficult prediction is regarding the course any Supreme Court will follow. The seventeen years of the Burger Court were not a time of judicial counterrevolution, as feared by liberals. The Supreme Court did not become reactionary, but instead adopted a middle course which confirmed the trends of late twentieth century jurisprudence. In one of history's ironies, decisions by this Court helped to end the Nixon Presidency.

Warren Burger was born on September 17, 1907, in St. Paul, Minnesota, into a large Swiss-German family of modest means. He attended public schools, worked his way through college at night, and then attended the St. Paul College of Law (Mitchell College of Law). Despite having to sell life insurance to finance his education, he graduated from law school *magna cum laude* in 1931. Burger married Elvira Stromberg in November, 1933, and the couple had two children. By 1935, Burger established himself as partner of a law firm where he practiced until 1953. During these years he taught law at his alma mater, participated in several of Harold Stassen's campaigns, and developed a lifelong appreciation for art and fine wines. His Washington career began in 1953, when he accepted a position as assistant attorney general, and, in 1956 President Eisenhower appointed him to the District of Columbia Circuit Court of Appeals. On that bench, he gained a reputation as a judge who was tough on criminals and who read the Constitution narrowly. He opposed the liberalization of criminal procedures mandated by the Warren Court both as an unjustified burden on the efficient prosecution of felons and as certain to clog court dockets across America. This latter concern reflected Burger's abiding interest in judicial administration, a cause he continued to espouse when chief justice. While on the Court of Appeals, he directed an

American Bar Association project on Minimum Standards for Criminal Justice, and helped to establish an Institute of Court Management to train officials who might relieve judges of administrative obligations. Although Burger was quietly prominent and committed to a conservative view of the Constitution, Nixon's nomination of him as chief justice on May 21, 1969 was unexpected since it was rumored the post would go to Attorney General Herbert Brownell. But, after only eighteen days, the Senate gave its consent, and on June 9, by a vote of 74-3, Warren Burger was named the fifteenth chief justice.

Before President Nixon completed three years in the White House, he was able to appoint three additional justices besides Burger to the Supreme Court. Many Republicans expected that the influx of conservative jurists would lead to a significant roll-back of the "ultra-liberal" decisions of the Warren Court; this proved a false dream. In regard to criminal justice issues, where Burger was on record as opposing *Miranda* and *Mapp*, the decisions of his Court largely sustained those precedents. Although Nixon had campaigned against a Supreme Court that was "weakening the peace forces and strengthening the criminal forces," the Burger Court upheld its predecessor's revolutionary attitude, while granting to police the benefit of the doubt in "gray areas." In law, the phrase *stare decisis* implies a respect for established law, and Burger's Court proved itself fundamentally conservative by respecting the decisions of the past. This attitude was reflected also in the continuing support that the justices gave to the campaign for racial equality. It was the Burger Court which upheld busing of students to end segregated schools in *Swann* (1971), declared constitutional affirmative action plans intended to compensate minorities for past discrimination in *Fullilove* (1980), and denied a tax exemption to a college with a racially biased admissions policy in *Bob Jones University* (1983). Since 1925, the Supreme Court has applied the Bill of Rights to the states by using the due process clause of the Fourteenth Amendment, and Burger's Court continued this process. A few analysts still believe that the Court unduly restricted constitutional liberties in a few cases, but, on the whole, citizens' rights were maintained and the First Amendment rights of the media were enhanced.

The Burger years provided the nation with moments of high legal drama as great decisions were announced. In 1973, *Roe v. Wade* declared that the right of privacy discovered in the Fourteenth Amendment during the Warren tenure did constitutionally protect a woman's decision whether or not to have an abortion; that ruling is still a matter of bitter national debate. Eighteen months later, with Chief Justice Burger speaking for a unanimous Court, *United States v. Nixon* ordered the president of the United States to comply with a subpoena ordering him to deliver to a special federal prosecutor conversations taped in the White House; the ruling virtually guaranteed Nixon's resignation. *Gregg v. Georgia* in 1976 reinstated the death penalty in the United States, and, under its auspices, over 140 executions have taken place in fifteen years. And finally, Burger's 1983 opinion in *INS v. Chadha* held the legislative veto to be unconstitutional, a single decision which invalidated more Congressional laws than in all previous Supreme Court history. Burger's "conservative" Court overruled more precedents, overturned more acts of Congress, and invalidated more state laws than its predecessor. Unlike Warren, Burger did not seem to be consciously inspired by a moral vision, but his Court cautiously, yet clearly, permitted the liberal trends of the past to continue.

No modern chief justice invested more time in working for judicial reform than did Warren Burger. His annual "State of the Judiciary" messages consistently challenged the legal profession to make better use of jurors, adopt procedures whereby a judge could control a case from start to finish, streamline the appeals route, and more effectively discipline lawyers. In 1972, he obtained an administrative assistant for the chief justice whose task was to organize reform suggestions, had many "hard sell" luncheons with the American Bar Association, and bombarded President Nixon with hand written memos suggesting changes. Burger wanted Congress to create a National Court of Appeals to screen circuit decisions as to their relevance and importance for the Supreme Court, but the proposal was not adopted. His constant desire to rationalize Court procedures led him to cut oral argument time before the justices to only thirty minutes, limit the length of documents and attorney briefs, install the Court's first computer system, and obtain three additional clerks for each justice. A traditionalist, Burger declared on November 15, 1984 "there will be no cameras in the Supreme Court of the United States while I sit there;" he thought publicity of any sort was "show business" that had no place in his court. But not even Burger's mania for order could impose discipline on a Court where plurality decisions with multiple concurrences seemed the rule. Burger led a bench less "social" than others, one that often resembled "nine law firms" each with a distinctive point of view. Case pressure left the justices with less time for consultations, and the result was a multiplicity of split decisions that often made the Court's opinion quite murky. Burger himself, it was whispered, added to the apparent disorder by making errors in the recording of votes. He steadfastly held that the seeming disarray merely reflected the difficulty of the cases and was a sign of the independence of mind that makes the Court unique.

Chief Justice Burger enjoyed the administration and ceremonial functions of his office. He was overjoyed to preside when Justice William Douglas broke the record for Court longevity in 1975, and he positively beamed when Sandra Day O'Conner became the first woman justice in 1981. Critics said Burger was late with his decisions, accused him of shifting his vote in order to retain the right to assign the opinion, and found him too willing to direct cases back to state courts. He simply shrugged off the barbs noting "it's a lot of fun" being chief. In May of 1986, he decided to leave the Court and accept the chairmanship of the National Commission honoring the Bicentennial of the Constitution; he was the sixth chief justice to resign. A year later on his eightieth birthday, September 17, 1987, he benignly presided over the 200th anniversary of the Constitution he had so well served. On June 25, 1995, Warren Earl Burger died of heart disease in his ninth year of retirement.

WILLIAM HUBBS REHNQUIST
October 1, 1924 – _ _ _ _
Chief Justice: September 26, 1986 - _ _ _ _

The political history of the United States in the 1980s was dominated by the avuncular figure of President Ronald Reagan. Like Richard Nixon before him, Reagan was partially elected because of his expressed anger at the trend of Supreme Court decisions over a generation, and his promise to name justices who would not attempt to legislate from the high bench. He offered the vision of a "social agenda" that could be implemented not only through government action, but also by favorable decisions from the more conservative Supreme Court he pledged to create by his appointments. Every president dreams of influencing history by naming a chief justice, but before the unexpected decision of Warren Burger to resign, it seemed that Reagan, a "lucky" President, would not be afforded that opportunity. Yet on June 17, 1986, Reagan announced not only the retirement of Burger but his choice for the new chief, Associate Justice William H. Rehnquist. A conservative, almost reactionary, jurist who had been on the Court since 1971, Rehnquist's reflexive rejection of federal authority seemed to fit the President's conception of the "proper role of the courts in our democratic system." It was a key appointment in Reagan's effort to restore the value system of an earlier America.

William Hubbs Rehnquist was born in Milwaukee, Wisconsin, October 1, 1924, and raised in the suburb of Shorewood. His father was a paper jobber whose brilliant son attended public schools before entering Kenyon College. Rehnquist served in the Air Force during World War II, then returned to school and received Stanford's B.A. and M.A. in 1948. He gained another M.A. from Harvard before entering Stanford Law School, where he graduated first in the class of 1952. Offered a Supreme Court clerkship by Justice Robert H. Jackson, Rehnquist quickly accepted and relocated to Washington, D.C. He married Natalie Corwell on August 29, 1953 and the couple has three children. While Jackson's clerk, Rehnquist wrote an internal memorandum which opposed judicial action to achieve racial desegregation, an analysis which became an issue years later during Rehnquist's confirmation hearings as associate justice, but the nominee has always asserted that the memo did not reflect his opinion, but was an effort to clarify the views of Justice Jackson. Many Rehnquist critics still believe the brief represented a clerk's attempt to dissuade Jackson from agreeing with *Brown v. Board of Education*. In 1953, Rehnquist moved to Arizona, where he founded his own law firm and participated in the right wing politics that characterized the state. He regularly denounced the liberal decisions of the Warren Court, participated in the Goldwater campaign of 1964, and ultimately returned to Washington as an assistant attorney general in the office of legal counsel. As an outspoken member of the Nixon administration from 1969 to 1971, Rehnquist stood out among conservatives for the rigidity of his beliefs and the ability with which he articulated them. On October 21, 1971, he was nominated to the Supreme Court by President Nixon, a forty-seven year old zealot who was expected to offer a "counterweight" to liberalism for at least a generation. Because of his right wing prominence, confirmation hearings before the Senate were quite strident and it was only by a vote of 68-26 that he won approval in December.

Rehnquist's career as an associate justice confirmed the expectations of both conservatives and liberals. He consistently voted to narrow federal authority and to permit the broadest possible latitude to state authority. He alone of the justices seemed consistently willing to rethink the prevailing truths accepted by the Court; *stare decisis* was less important to him than philosophical rightness. As a result, he often found himself a solitary dissenter in cases dealing with women's rights or the desegregation process. His clerks jokingly called him the "Lone Ranger," but his well written opinions gained him respect if not a following on the Court. He was one of only two dissenters in *Roe v. Wade.* In the Nixon tapes case, he recused himself, since he had a close professional relationship with at least three of the parties to the suit. Occasionally, he was able to speak for the Court, as he did in *National League of Cities v. Usery* in 1976, which protected states from extended federal wage and hour provisions. But, more generally, his narrow construction of the Constitution and the Bill of Rights made him the most predictable vote and most frequent dissenter on the Burger Court.

Rehnquist's nomination as chief justice engendered another bitter round of Senate confirmation hearings. Liberals opposed his constitutional philosophy, but unexpected Republican opposition surfaced because of Rehnquist's failure to disqualify himself in a 1972 case. In the end, although more negative votes were cast against his confirmation than any successful nominee in Court history, Reagan's choice won approval by a vote of 65-33. Rehnquist took the oath as chief justice on September 26, 1986, the same day another conservative justice, Antonin Scalia, was also sworn in. So far, the major shift that conservatives expected in Court opinions has not taken place. Rehnquist has written of his belief that Warren Burger was happy at his succession, but the same institutional dynamics that his predecessor encountered seem to have tempered the new chief's militant conservatism. Since the chief justice "leads by example," Rehnquist has admitted that he is "more punctual" in attending sessions and in convening the conference. He has written a book on the history of the Court and has become more mindful of its institutional importance. Rehnquist's opinion for the court in *Hustler v. Falwell (1988)*, surprised observers of the Court, for it showed a willingness on his part to move away from earlier positions even on such a "litmus test" issue as pornography when it involved the First Amendment. Speaking for a unanimous Court, Rehnquist extended the protection for speech relative to public figures even if the criticism involved was outrageous. A reverence for the Bill of Rights was also demonstrated by the Court's handling of flagburning cases in 1989-1990, cases which found Rehnquist in the minority. With other rulings, however, it does appear that the long predicted rightward tilt of the Court is occurring as significant limitations were placed on civil rights proceedings and affirmative action programs. Although it is far too early to characterize his tenure as chief justice, but it is interesting to note that Rehnquist delivered a speech in 1984 in which he said that presidents who attempt to reshape the Supreme Court by their appointments usually are disappointed.

The greatest challenge any chief justice faces is the need to mobilize his Court, and it was the dream of conservatives that Rehnquist's installation might herald a bench reminiscent of the 1920s or even the 1890s. Militating against such unity of viewpoint has been the daunting multiplicity of opinions that the modern Court, "nine law firms," seems to produce. The new chief believes his Court is "stretched quite thin trying to do what we ought to do" to review and decide cases. He endorses limiting time for oral argument, since any good lawyer ought to make his point in thirty minutes. Although he has adopted an abbreviated conference style, nothing seems capable of limiting the many opinions those conferences produce. But if opinions are more complicated, there are fewer of them because a downward trend in cases has been apparent since 1988. Yet, despite fewer and longer decisions, Court analysts agreed that Rehnquist had failed to build a stable majority reflective of his conservative philosophy before the presidency of Bill Clinton.

Chief Justice Rehnquist's consitutional views favored Executive power, showed deference towards police authority, would enhance states rights and the protections given to private property and would have eased federal civil rights mandates. But 1994 Court decisions in these areas were decidedly mixed. Rehnquist has strongly advocated limitations on the use of *habeas corpus,* and his *Brecht* opinion in 1993 ordered federal courts to allow procedural appeals only in cases where "a substantial and injurious effect" on the verdict could be shown. Moreover, his Court has proven to be

ever more reluctant to approve multiple appeals in capital punishment cases. Not until the 1994-95 term, however, did other justices
seem ready to follow their Chief towards a more conservative view
of the Constitution. Perhaps most significant was Rehnquist's
majority opinion in *United States v. Lopez* which, for the first time in
60 years, invalidated a federal law as exceeding the bounds of the
commerce clause. *Lopez* clearly limited the authority of Congress
and conservatives trumpeted that it signified an important shift in
the Court's attitude. Later decisions in the 1995 term, *Adarand v.
Pena, Missouri v. Jenkins* and *Miller v. Johnson* were each in turn
hailed as evidence of the long expected Rehnquist transformation,
but the truth of this assertion is yet to be determined. In a larger
sense, a decade of Rehnquist leadership had more often disappointed the expectations of conservatives. His Court had not
reversed any of the landmark decisions of the past thirty years, and
the mandates of *Baker, Miranda, Bakke* and *Roe* stood with only
minor alterations. Under its sixteenth chief justice, the High Bench
had not yet reversed the liberal jurisprudence of a generation. The
Supreme Court continues to be the most respected branch of the
American government, in part because it provides a sense of stability in our tumultuous society.

THE JUSTICES OF THE
UNITED STATES SUPREME COURT

Justice	State	Appointed by	Term	Life Span
John Jay	N.Y.	Washington	1789-1795	1745-1829
John Rutledge	S.C.	Washington	1789-1791	1739-1800
William Cushing	Mass.	Washington	1789-1810	1732-1810
James Wilson	Pa.	Washington	1789-1798	1742-1798
John Blair	Va.	Washington	1789-1796	1732-1800
James Iredell	N.C.	Washington	1790-1799	1751-1799
Thomas Johnson *Replaced Rutledge*	Md.	Washington	1791-1793	1732-1819
William Paterson *Replaced Johnson*	N.J.	Washington	1793-1806	1745-1806
John Rutledge *Replaced Jay*	S.C.	Washington	1795	1739-1800
Samuel Chase *Replaced Blair*	Md.	Washington	1796-1811	1741-1811
Oliver Ellsworth *Replaced Rutledge*	Conn.	Washington	1796-1800	1745-1807
Bushrod Washington *Replaced Wilson*	Va.	John Adams	1798-1829	1762-1829
Alfred Moore *Replaced Iredell*	N.C.	John Adams	1799-1804	1755-1810
John Marshall *Replaced Ellsworth*	Va.	John Adams	1801-1835	1755-1835
William Johnson *Replaced Moore*	S.C.	Jefferson	1804-1834	1771-1834
H. Brockholst Livingston *Replaced Paterson*	N.Y.	Jefferson	1806-1823	1757-1823
Thomas Todd	Ky.	Jefferson	1807-1826	1765-1826
Gabriel Duvall *Replaced Chase*	Md.	Madison	1811-1835	1752-1844
Joseph Story *Replaced Cushing*	Mass.	Madison	1811-1845	1799-1845
Smith Thompson *Replaced Livingstone*	N.Y.	Monroe	1823-1843	1768-1843
Robert Trimble *Replaced Todd*	Ky.	John Quincy Adams	1826-1828	1776-1828
John McLean *Replaced Trimble*	Ohio	Jackson	1829-1861	1785-1861
Henry Baldwin *Replaced Washington*	Pa.	Jackson	1830-1844	1780-1844

Justice	State	Appointed by	Term	Life Span
James M. Wayne	Ga.	Jackson	1835-1867	1790-1867
Replaced Johnson				
Roger B. Taney	Md.	Jackson	1836-1864	1777-1864
Replaced Marshall				
Philip P. Barbour	Va.	Jackson	1836-1841	1783-1841
Replaced Duvall				
John Catron	Tenn.	Van Buren	1837-1865	1786-1865
John McKinley	Ala.	Van Buren	1837-1852	1780-1852
Peter V. Daniel	Va.	Van Buren	1841-1860	1784-1860
Replaced Barbour				
Samuel Nelson	N.Y.	Tyler	1845-1872	1792-1873
Replaced Thompson				
Levi Woodbury	N.H.	Polk	1845-1851	1789-1851
Replaced Story				
Robert C. Grier	Pa.	Polk	1846-1870	1794-1870
Replaced Baldwin				
Benjamin R. Curtis	Mass.	Fillmore	1851-1857	1809-1874
Replaced Woodbury				
John A. Campbell	Ala.	Pierce	1853-1861	1811-1889
Replaced McKinley				
Nathan Clifford	Maine	Buchanan	1858-1881	1803-1881
Replaced Curtis				
Noah H. Swayne	Ohio	Lincoln	1862-1881	1804-1884
Replaced McLean				
Samuel F. Miller	Iowa	Lincoln	1862-1890	1816-1890
Replaced Daniel				
David Davis	Ill.	Lincoln	1862-1877	1815-1886
Replaced Campbell				
Stephen J. Field	Calif.	Lincoln	1863-1897	1816-1899
Salmon P. Chase	Ohio	Lincoln	1864-1873	1808-1873
Replaced Taney				
William Strong	Pa.	Grant	1870-1880	1808-1895
Replaced Grier				
Joseph P. Bradley	N.J.	Grant	1870-1892	1813-1892
Ward Hunt	N.Y.	Grant	1872-1882	1820-1886
Replaced Nelson				
Morrison R. Waite	Ohio	Grant	1874-1888	1816-1888
Replaced Chase				
John Marshall Harlan	Ky.	Hayes	1877-1911	1833-1911
Replaced Davis				
William B. Woods	Ga.	Hayes	1880-1887	1824-1887
Replaced Strong				
Stanley Matthews	Ohio	Garfield	1881-1889	1824-1889
Replaced Swayne				

Justice	State	Appointed by	Term	Life Span
Horace Gray *Replaced Clifford*	Mass.	Arthur	1881-1902	1828-1902
Samuel Blatchford *Replaced Hunt*	N.Y.	Arthur	1882-1893	1820-1893
Lucius Q. C. Lamar *Replaced Woods*	Miss.	Cleveland	1888-1893	1825-1893
Melville W. Fuller *Replaced Waite*	Ill.	Cleveland	1888-1910	1833-1910
David J. Brewer *Replaced Matthews*	Kan.	Benjamin Harrison	1889-1910	1837-1910
Henry B. Brown *Replaced Miller*	Mich.	Benjamin Harrison	1890-1906	1836-1913
George Shiras *Replaced Bradley*	Pa.	Benjamin Harrison	1892-1903	1832-1924
Howell E. Jackson *Replaced Lamar*	Tenn.	Benjamin Harrison	1893-1895	1832-1895
Edward D. White *Replaced Blatchford*	La.	Cleveland	1894-1910	1845-1921
Rufus W. Peckham *Replaced Jackson*	N.Y.	Cleveland	1895-1909	1838-1909
Joseph McKenna *Replaced Field*	Calif.	McKinley	1898-1925	1843-1926
Oliver Wendell Holmes *Replaced Gray*	Mass.	Theodore Roosevelt	1902-1932	1841-1935
William R. Day *Replaced Shiras*	Ohio	Theodore Roosevelt	1903-1922	1849-1923
William H. Moody *Replaced Brown*	Mass.	Theodore Roosevelt	1906-1910	1853-1917
Horace H. Lurton *Replaced Peckham*	Tenn.	Taft	1909-1914	1844-1914
Charles E. Hughes *Replaced Brewer*	N.Y.	Taft	1910-1916	1862-1948
Edward D. White *Replaced Fuller*	La.	Taft	1910-1921	1845-1921
Willis Van Devanter *Replaced White*	Wy.	Taft	1910-1937	1859-1941
Joseph R. Lamar *Replaced Moody*	Ga.	Taft	1910-1916	1857-1916
Mahlon Pitney *Replaced Harlan*	N.J.	Taft	1912-1922	1858-1924
James C. McReynolds *Replaced Lurton*	Tenn.	Wilson	1914-1941	1862-1946
Louis D. Brandeis *Replaced Lamar*	Mass.	Wilson	1916-1939	1856-1941

Justice	State	Appointed by	Term	Life Span
John H. Clarke *Replaced Hughes*	Ohio	Wilson	1916-1922	1857-1945
William H. Taft *Replaced White*	Conn.	Harding	1921-1930	1857-1930
George Sutherland *Replaced Clarke*	Utah	Harding	1922-1938	1862-1942
Pierce Butler *Replaced Day*	Minn.	Harding	1922-1939	1866-1939
Edward T. Sanford *Replaced Pitney*	Tenn.	Harding	1923-1930	1865-1930
Harlan F. Stone *Replaced McKenna*	N.Y.	Coolidge	1925-1941	1872-1946
Charles F. Hughes *Replaced Taft*	N.Y.	Hoover	1930-1941	1862-1948
Owen J. Roberts *Replaced Sanford*	Pa.	Hoover	1930-1945	1875-1955
Benjamin N. Cardozo *Replaced Holmes*	N.Y.	Hoover	1932-1938	1870-1938
Hugo L. Black *Replaced Van Devanter*	Ala.	Franklin D. Roosevelt	1937-1971	1886-1971
Stanley F. Reed *Replaced Sutherland*	Ky.	Franklin D. Roosevelt	1938-1957	1884-1980
Felix Frankfurter *Replaced Cardozo*	Mass.	Franklin D. Roosevelt	1939-1962	1882-1965
William O. Douglas *Replaced Brandeis*	Conn.	Franklin D. Roosevelt	1939-1975	1898-1980
Frank Murphy *Replaced Butler*	Mich.	Franklin D. Roosevelt	1940-1949	1890-1949
James F. Byrnes *Replaced McReynolds*	S.C.	Franklin D. Roosevelt	1941-1942	1879-1972
Harlan F. Stone *Replaced Hughes*	N.Y.	Franklin D. Roosevelt	1941-1946	1872-1946
Robert H. Jackson *Replaced Stone*	N.Y.	Franklin D. Roosevelt	1941-1954	1892-1954
Wiley H. Rutledge *Replaced Byrnes*	Iowa	Franklin D. Roosevelt	1943-1949	1894-1949
Harold H. Burton *Replaced Roberts*	Ohio	Truman	1945-1958	1888-1964
Frederick M. Vinson *Replaced Stone*	Ky.	Truman	1946-1953	1890-1953
Tom C. Clark *Replaced Murphy*	Tex.	Truman	1949-1967	1899-1977
Sherman Minton *Replaced Rutledge*	Ind.	Truman	1949-1956	1890-1965

Justice	State	Appointed by	Term	Life Span
Earl Warren *Replaced Vinson*	Calif.	Eisenhower	1953-1969	1891-1974
John Marshall Harlan *Replaced Jackson*	N.Y.	Eisenhower	1955-1971	1899-1971
William J. Brennan, Jr. *Replaced Minton*	N.J.	Eisenhower	1957-1990	1906-
Charles E. Whittaker *Replaced Reed*	Mo.	Eisenhower	1957-1962	1901-1973
Potter Stewart *Replaced Burton*	Ohio	Eisenhower	1958-1981	1915-1985
Byron R. White *Replaced Whittaker*	Colo.	Kennedy	1962-1993	1917-
Arthur J. Goldberg *Replaced Frankfurter*	Ill.	Kennedy	1962-1965	1908-1990
Abe Fortas *Replaced Goldburg*	Tenn.	Lyndon B. Johnson	1965-1969	1910-1982
Thurgood Marshall *Replaced Clark*	Md.	Lyndon B. Johnson	1967-1991	1908-1993
Warren E. Burger *Replaced Warren*	Minn.	Nixon	1969-1986	1907-1995
Harry A. Blackmun *Replaced Fortas*	Minn.	Nixon	1970-	1908-
Lewis F. Powell, Jr. *Replaced Black*	Va.	Nixon	1972-1987	1907
William H. Rehnquist *Replaced Harlan*	Ariz.	Nixon	1972-1986	1924
John Paul Stevens *Replaced Douglas*	Ill.	Ford	1975-	1920-
Sandra Day O'Connor *Replaced Stewart*	Ariz.	Reagan	1981-	1930-
William H. Rehnquist *Replaced Burger*	Ariz.	Reagan	1986-	1924-
Antonin Scalia *Replaced Rehnquist*	N.J.	Reagan	1986-	1936-
Anthony M. Kennedy *Replaced Powell*	Calif.	Reagan	1987-	1936-
David Souter *Replaced Brennan*	N.H.	Bush	1990-	1939-
Clarence Thomas *Replaced Marshall*	Ga.	Bush	1991-	1948-
Ruth Bader Ginsberg *Replaced White*	N.Y.	Clinton	1993-	1933-
Stephen Breyer *Replaced Blackman*	Ma.	Clinton	1994-	1938-

THE POWER OF
JUDICIAL REVIEW

The Supreme Court of the United States is quite simply the most powerful judicial body in the history of the world. The primary reason for this eminence is its power of judicial review over the legislation passed by Congress and the enactments of the various states of the Union. It is the privilege of interpreting the Constitution, the right to decide on its meaning, which sets the Court apart from all others and has given it a pivotal role in national history. But judicial review is not expressly voiced or granted in the Constitution itself. How the Court achieved its right to interpret the 7,000 words of the constitution is one of the most vital stories of American history.

The concept of the "judicial review" of legislation to determine its legitimacy had been debated in legal circles for many years before the Founding Fathers met in Philadelphia to draft the Constitution. In New York during the 1780s, Alexander Hamilton had once argued that a legislative act was void because it was in violation of John Jay's Constitution, but the presiding state judge had rejected his reasoning. Hamilton's *Federalist*, nevertheless, made the same argument regarding the implicit powers of a national judiciary. Nationalists found justification for judicial review in the Constitution's Article VI, which declares the document "shall be the supreme law of the land." Although the delegates at Philadelphia failed to expressly grant judicial review to the new Supreme Court, most scholars agree that they expected that still uncreated body to review legislation. Laws do not write themselves, enforce themselves, or interpret themselves and the tone of the Philadelphia debates implied that a court must be the final arbiter of meaning. At least twenty-five of the delegates to the Convention are known to have supported some type of judicial review, and Max Farrand's *Records of the Federal Convention* could discover only two who expressed reservations. The rest, it seems, either had no opinion or willingly left the issue to the determination of the men who would form the new government. One strong negative proof of judicial review's acceptance was the Convention's refusal to approve a Council of Revision in which members of the judicial arm would join with the executive to veto acts of Congress. The delegates seemingly preferred a separation of authority that would permit the Court to render a final yes or no decision on the legitimacy of legislation. Moreover, it may be remembered that future Chief Justices Ellsworth and Marshall both specifically endorsed the concept of judicial review during the ratification battles in their respective states. Finally, common sense itself suggests that because courts, by their very nature, reconcile conflicts on the meaning of law, they must possess the authority to decide what law prevails in a dispute.

It is easy to assert that the Supreme Court probably held the right of judicial review, but it still had to be won in law and prac- tice. It was during the 1790s that Supreme Court justices on their circuit duties first began to exercise that power, and they held state laws to be unconstitutional on at least four occasions. More- over, the justices of Jay's Court refused to abide by the terms of a Congressional statute which mandated their sitting as commis- sioners to settle pension claims by veterans of the Revolution. Since the justices agreed to do so voluntarily, Congress revoked the law and so avoided an early test of the principle of judicial review. In 1796, the Court in *Hylton v. United States* held that a tax on carriages was valid, but since the law was upheld there was lit- tle comment. Thus, even before the advent of John Marshall, there had been instances of judicial review of both state and Con- gressional laws, even though the Court had not yet taken the ulti- mate step of declaring an act of Congress invalid.

That step would be taken in the case of *Marbury v. Madison*, by most assessments the single most important case in Supreme Court history. *Marbury* is also an ideal example of how political considerations can enter into the decisions of the high bench. The case arose after the Federalists lost the bitter Presidential campaign of 1800 to Thomas Jefferson and his Republican Party. Desperate to maintain their philosophical hold on at least one branch of the government, the Federalists enacted the Judiciary Act (February 13, 1801), and the Act Concerning the District of Columbia (February 27, 1801), which permitted President Adams to pack the circuit court system and the newly occupied federal district with quickly appointed "midnight judges." These officials presumably would protect Federalist principles until the party's electoral fortunes improved. John Marshall, who had taken his seat on the Supreme Court only on February 4th, was not one of these new appointees. Since he continued to act as Secretary of State for the dying administration, however, it was his duty to deliver commissions of appointment to the new judges once he had affixed to them the Great Seal of the United States. Until its last day in power, the Federalist Senate was approving presidential appointments, the president was signing them, and Marshall was completing the paperwork and sending them to the new officials. His failure to do so in the case of William Marbury, named justice of the peace in the District of Columbia, was the reason that the case came before the Supreme Court.

When the Republicans took power, Jefferson and his Secretary of State, James Madison, discovered that not all new certificates of appointment had been delivered. Marbury, who knew of his appointment, asked Madison to deliver his document, but the new secretary refused. The would-be justice of the peace then asked the Supreme Court to issue a writ of *mandamus*, an order requiring government officials to perform their sworn duty. Marshall, in December, 1801, asked Madison to show cause why the Court should not issue the order. There the process suddenly halted because, early in 1802, the Republican Congress repealed the Federalist laws and so abolished the judgeships they had authorized. Moreover, the new judiciary statute ordered sitting justices of the Supreme Court to resume circuit riding duty and eliminated the upcoming term of the court. Since his Court could not meet until February, 1803, Marshall used the interim to forge a strategy that would guarantee the role of the judicial branch of the government in American life. Accepting political reality, Marshall and his brethren agreed in the *Laird* decision that it was within the prerogative of the Congress to order Supreme Court justices to ride circuit and to dismiss the new circuit court appointees. The Jeffersonians savored their triumph, knowing that only Marbury's petition for a writ was still pending, and that case was almost moot since his unfilled term as justice of the peace was about to expire. Marbury's cause was of so little importance to the administration that it did not even bother to appear in Marshall's Court to argue against the issuance of a writ with which the president would never comply.

Out of this unpromising situation, Marshall created constitutional history and the power of judicial review. His decision in *Marbury v. Madison* first asked if the petitioner was entitled to his commission. The answer was clearly yes. Once President Adams had signed it and the Secretary of State (Marshall himself) recorded it, the appointment was legitimate and Madison had no right to withhold it. Marbury had obviously sustained a civil injury and, in the United States, "a government of laws, and not of men," he had rightly come to the Court to obtain *mandamus*. Marshall knew that the Court had issued such writs in the 1790s, but he also understood that the Republicans would ignore his order to deliver the commission. Non-compliance would demonstrate the weakness of the Court in relation to the executive and denigrate the law itself. Therefore, Marshall concluded his opinion by saying that, although Marbury deserved his commission and the Republicans (including President Jefferson) were wrong to deny it to him, the Supreme Court did not have the authority to issue the writ. The Judiciary Act of 1789, drafted by Senator Ellsworth, had unconstitutionally expanded the jurisdiction of the Supreme Court because its Section 13 had given it the right to issue writs of *mandamus* to officers of the government. "It is a proposition too plain to be contested," wrote Marshall, "that the constitution controls any legislative act repugnant to it" and, since Section 13 was in violation of Article III of the Constitution, it was void. The chief justice asserted that "It is, emphatically, the province and duty of the judicial department to say what the law is" and, to do this, they must examine the meaning of the Constitution. In *Marbury* the Court declared that an act of Congress had unconstitutionally expanded the power of the third branch beyond the limits set by the Constitution. Marshall had given the Jeffersonians their victory, but it was a phyrric one over *Marbury* alone. A small part of a Federalist law had been invalidated, the Court had lost a minor bit of its authority, but the right of the institution to interpret the meaning of the Constitution had been affirmed. Never again would Marshall find an act of Congress to be unconstitutional. Over the next three decades, Marshall used the awesome power of review to enhance the prestige of the national government. *Marbury* was both politically astute and an institutional *coup de main*. By side-stepping a confrontation with the Republicans, Marshall gave them a meaningless victory, but achieved for his Court the final say over state and federal legislation. *Marbury* represents judicial statesmanship and institutional aggrandizement of the highest order and is fundamental to the role that the Supreme Court has played in the life of the nation.

THE SIZE OF THE
SUPREME COURT

Contemporary Americans are often confounded when they discover that the Supreme Court has not always consisted of nine judges, a number that they assume is written into the Constitution. But the Constitution merely empowered Congress to establish the Court; it was Congress that decided upon its original size, and it was Congress that has altered it many times over the course of American history. Analyzing changes in the number of justices authorized illustrates how closely tied to politics the judicial process has always been in this nation, and puts an end to the myth that the Supreme Court is totally removed from and unaffected by governmental change.

The organization of the third branch of the new republican government of the United States was first provided for in the Judiciary Act of 1789. A Supreme Court consisting of a chief justice and five associates was authorized, and the nation was divided into thirteen judicial districts, one for each state. Three circuit courts were created from the thirteen districts, each presided over by a panel of two justices of the Supreme Court sitting with a district judge. This was the "circuit riding" obligation that Jay's Court found so obnoxious and vehemently protested against without gaining relief. Presidents Washington and Adams were able to staff all these courts with loyal Federalists during the first decade of America's existence under the Constitution, and the general tenor of judicial decisions was suitably nationalistic and gratifying. But the loss of the presidency and Congress to the Jeffersonians in the elections of 1800 panicked the Federalists. In February, 1801, as the Adams administration faced its end, the outgoing Federalist Congress approved a Judiciary Act which created sixteen circuit courts needing additional judges, having enlarged jurisdiction, and demanding the appointment of new federal attorneys, marshals, and court personnel. The act absolved Supreme Court judges from "riding circuit" and changed the number of justices from six to five at the next vacancy. Although the act did make needed reforms in the court system, its overtly partisan purpose was to pack the judicial branch with Federalists and deny Jefferson any Supreme Court appointment until there were two vacant seats. We have seen how Adams' naming of the "midnight judges" led to *Marbury,* but it first provoked the Republicans to repeal the 1801 law and create six circuit courts (each staffed by one Supreme Court justice and a district judge). The Judiciary Act of 1802 reconstituted the Supreme Court to six members, (it never had fallen to five), and its judges were again asked to perform circuit duty. Indeed, it was not until 1891 that the obligation of "riding the circuit" was lifted from the justices of the high court.

One of Thomas Jefferson's most enduring frustrations was that his administration was unable to make any major impact on Federalist control of the judiciary. These were years in which John Marshall transformed the Court from weakness into a strong agency reflective of his will. Jefferson's first two appointees became incorporated in that judicial phalanx. The pace of Court work was increasing, however, and, in 1807, the Jeffersonians passed another Judiciary Act raising Supreme Court membership to seven; they also added a seventh circuit to handle states west of the Appalachians. Thomas Jefferson's third Court nomination was subsequently made, but failed to alter the dominance of Marshall and his principles. Jefferson's three successors each asked Congress to enlarge the Court in order to acknowledge the growth of America to the south and west and to alleviate the burden of circuit riding. Congress failed to act because it did not wish any incumbent president to have the privilege of extra Court nominations, but the Democrats of 1837 had no such qualms about Andrew Jackson. They presented him with a bill raising the number of justices to nine and the president, having signed the bill, immediately made two nominations to the Court. Both won Senate approval, although one subsequently refused to serve.

The Court remained fixed at nine justices for another generation until the nation faced the trauma of the Civil War. The admission of California necessitated that another circuit be established for the west coast (1855), and inevitably pressure mounted to expand the Supreme Court. President Abraham Lincoln's liberal use of executive authority in fighting the war had made some of his actions legally suspect and, although he had made three appointments to the Court by 1863, his war making abilities were still insecure. The Republicans met that crisis by adding a tenth seat to the Court, thus providing another nomination to the President. When the bloody Civil War ended, the Radical Congress was hardly so accommodating toward Lincoln's successor. Andrew Johnson was looked upon as an impediment to the successful Reconstruction of the Union. Therefore, in 1866, the Congress cut the size of the Court from ten to seven in order to prevent the president from filling Court seats with men whose views might be unreliable. The statute prevented Johnson from making any appointments to the Court during his three years in office, and the high bench had fallen to eight justices when his term ended in 1869. Less than a month later, the Congress made its last adjustment in the size of the Supreme Court. The election of Ulysses S. Grant to the presidency guaranteed that the Radical viewpoint would be respectfully heard in the White House, and so the Judiciary Act of April 10, 1869, raised the Court to nine justices. An unexpected resignation provided Grant with the opportunity to make two quick nominations, a occurrence of critical importance in economic history since paper currency was declared legal payment for all contracts only by virtue of those two votes. Grant was naturally accused by his opponents of "packing" the Court, but most scholars find the charge less than convincing.

For over a century, the number of seats on the Court has held steady at nine, despite arguments that its size ought to be adjusted to reflect the responsibilities of a world power. By far the most significant of these efforts came in 1937 when President Franklin D. Roosevelt, who had just won an overwhelming reelection to the White House, proposed a "Court reform" scheme which would have permitted him to name up to six additional justices. Roosevelt's plan suggested that he be given the right to nominate a new judge, up to a maximum of fifteen justices, for every Supreme Court justice over the age of 70 who chose not to retire. Although he presented the idea as a means of increasing the efficiency of the Court, it was clear to both politicians and the public that the president was seeking to punish the "nine old men" of a "horse and buggy court" that had declared unconstitutional large parts of his New Deal. To his many critics, Roosevelt intended to "pack" the Court with liberal justices loyal to himself. Even presidential defenders had difficulty supporting a plan that seemed a naked executive attack upon the independence of the third branch of government. When Chief Justice Charles Evans Hughes released a letter asserting that the Court was fully up to date on its calendar, and claiming that additional justices would only delay decisions by increasing the deliberation time for each case, the president's cause was dealt a mortal blow. Equally telling was a series of Court decisions in the spring of 1937 that upheld critical New Deal legislation, a reversal of attitude which led many to suggest that the justices had "read the election returns." In either case, the "packing" plan died an unlamented death, and natural turnover on the Court soon permitted Roosevelt to nominate liberal justices to replace the conservative "Four Horsemen" who had opposed his legislative initiatives. Many believe that the President lost the battle but won the war; Yet, in a larger sense, the Court as an institution won for its independence was maintained even in the face of a hostile executive at the height of his influence.

The shifting size of the Court over two centuries indicates not only that Congress has utilized its constitutional right to alter the bench but also that political motivations have never been foreign to the operation of the judicial branch. From the time of Washington, presidents have sought to achieve through their nominations to the Court a judiciary which is philosophically compatible. The goal of any executive is not total control, but the ability to influence the future through his selections. The Senate has recognized this executive aim, and has used its constitutional right to "advise and consent" to reject over a fifth of all Court nominations. Such battles have been less frequent in the twentieth century, but the Senate rejection of President Reagan's nomination of Robert Bork to the Supreme Court indicates that the "checks and balances" built into the constitutional process still apply. The Founding Fathers, wherever they may be, probably nodded sagely, for that tension between the branches is exactly the way they intended the Constitution to operate. A century of tradition today sets the number of Supreme Court Justices at nine, but the battle over the meaning of the Constitution continues.

HOME FOR THE
SUPREME COURT

A typical contemporary visitor to Washington, D.C., normally finds the time to spend a few precious minutes standing before or wandering through the great marble-faced building from which the Supreme Court issues its decisions. With his back to the Capitol, our tourist can almost feel the tensions that have often flowed between these two centers of power, vibrations altered, yet intensified, by those emanating from the White House almost a mile away. One can perhaps be forgiven for thinking that the constitutional balance between the three branches is somehow mirrored in the different structures that house them, and that it has always been so. Yet, the fact is that the Supreme Court, Hamilton's "least dangerous branch," was, until half a century ago, an institution without a home of its own. Fittingly, the judiciary did not gain its own quarters until America was deep into this most litigious of our centuries.

Senator Ellsworth's Judiciary Act (1789) established the court system, but made no provision for a meeting place for the Supreme Court. Presumably Chief Justice Jay made the arrangements for his Court's inaugural session, scheduled for February 1, 1790, in the Royal Exchange on Broad Street, New York City. An open-air market filled the first floor of the cupola-crested structure, but on its second floor was a sixty foot long room with a vaulted ceiling which had been used for meetings and exhibitions. On February 2nd, when a quorum of four judges was present, the first session was held, and the Court made a splendid show in its black or scarlet robes and optional English wig. But there was no business beyond organizational chores, and the Court adjourned after a week. A second term, August 2-3, was no more active, and then the Court prepared to join the government's move from its temporary capital to Philadelphia, where it spent the next decade. After its February, 1791, session held in Independence Hall, the Court sat regularly in the new City Hall, where it shared a room with the mayor's court; it was here that the first decisions of Jay's Court were made. Most attention centered on the west wing of the City Hall where Congress met, and few noticed or cared that three August terms of the Supreme Court had to be cancelled because of outbreaks of yellow fever in the river city. More respect and a better location were expected when the government moved to the Federal District under construction along the Potomac.

In December, 1800, the transfer from Philadelphia to Washington took place, a move from America's largest and most cosmopolitan city to a wilderness village of mud and crudity. Almost a decade after George Washington had designated the site, Pierre Charles L'Enfant's city plan was still in its earliest phases. The first stage of the Capitol had been completed, however, and a large White House for the Executive was almost ready for occupancy by President and Mrs. Adams. A site designated for the Court remained swampy and covered with brush, perhaps an indication of L'Enfant's scorn for John Jay. In another planning snub of the Court, our capital city of so many lettered avenues does not have one for the letter "J," permanent proof of L'Enfant's dislike for the first chief justice. A Court without accommodations had to go begging, and Congress made available a small committee room in the east wing. In that tiny chamber, only 24 by 30 feet, John Marshall took his oath. Over the next few years, the Court occupied several basement rooms until Capitol architect Benjamin Latrobe suggested they move into the "library formerly occupied by the House." After two sessions there, the justices found it so cold and forbidding that they chose to hold their 1809 sessions in Long's Tavern; typically a Jeffersonian Congress had not bothered to appropriate money for Court renovations. Not until February, 1810, did the Court ever have a room designed for its use, and, even then, it had to share the facility with the U.S. Circuit Court and the Orphan's Court. The chamber had been used by the Senate until 1807, but now became home to the Court.

The sense of security and place lasted only four years. The War of 1812 turned into a military fiasco and, on August 24, 1814, the victorious British army burned the Capitol, supposedly using Supreme Court documents to start the blaze. Again, Marshall's Court was forced to wander – first to the "Brick Capitol," for two years in a private house, to "a dungeon" in the bowels of a rebuilding Capitol – until the old Senate chamber was fully repaired in 1819. Many doubted that the room was worthy of a bench that announced *Dartmouth* and *McCullough* there, but it remained home to the Court until 1860. Some reporters described its location as the end of a labyrinth, but four decades of legal history were made in a space so small that the justices had to robe in the sight of spectators. If the modern tourist enters the Capitol today, he can see this chamber as it appeared in the 1850s, for it was restored for the Bicentennial celebrations. After forty years in the basement, continuing construction of the Capitol made it possible for the Court to move upstairs and, in 1860, it took over premises which the Senate had used since 1819. The chamber was 75 by 45 feet and had a skylight that made everyone feel "calm and peaceful." For the next seventy-five years, the decisions of the Court were issued from an area in which there was never sufficient room for offices, dining facilities, library books or conferences. These were inconveniences, but perhaps the worst indignity was that the judiciary remained a guest of the legislative branch.

The man most responsible for altering the situation was William Howard Taft, who advocated a separate building for the Court even during his presidency. As chief justice, Taft insisted that the judicial branch must have its own quarters, even though he knew that Fuller's Court had unanimously rejected a move to the Congressional Library Building in 1896. Not until 1929 was he able to overcome all obstacles and win a $10,000,000 appropriation from a reluctant Congress. The site selected for the Court's home was across the plaza from the modern Capitol, 1 First Street NE, where the "Brick Capitol" had once housed Congress. There a "Marble Temple" designed by Cass Gilbert in Greek Corinthian style rapidly rose; at a final cost of $9,740,000, the Supreme Court entered its first real home on October 7, 1935. It is only fair to say that not all the justices were pleased. Chief Justice Hughes, who had fought hard for its completion, thought of it only as "a place to hang my hat," and one of his colleagues asked if the Court was expected to enter riding nine elephants. Future Chief Justice Stone was reported to have described his brethren as resembling "nine black beetles in the temple of Karnak." Despite the elegance of their new surroundings, it was not until after World War II that all the justices agreed to regularly work there. Nevertheless, it contains all the facilities that the Court needs, including a gymnasium which has been called the highest court in the land. In recent times the Court has been fully computerized under the leadership of Chief Justice Burger. Now that the marble temple has been home to the Court for 55 years, our tourist may legitimately look on it with a great deal of awe. The venue of our Supreme Court seems at last to be a fitting monument to the constitutional history of the nation. From this massive structure come the decisions that permit Americans to believe in the words enshrined over its entrance, "Equal Justice Under Law."

FOR FURTHER READING

Scholars and lawyers love to write about the Supreme Court, its justices, and the impact that constitutional decisions have made on American life. Libraries are full of these volumes, and the listing below is designed to further the interested reader's understanding of an individual chief justice or the workings of the Court. This bibliography is by no means exhaustive, but illustrates the rich resources available to anyone concerned with the constitutional history of the United States.

Abraham, Henry J. *Justices and Presidents: A Political History of Political Appointments to the Supreme Court.* (New York: Oxford University Press, 1974).

Baker, Leonard. *Back to Back: The Duel Between F.D.R. and the Supreme Court.* (New York: Harper & Row, 1967).

___. *John Marshall: A Life in the Law.* (New York: Macmillan, 1974).

Barry, Richard. *Mr. Rutledge of South Carolina.* (New York: Duell, Sloan and Pearce, 1942).

Berger, Raoul. *Government by Judiciary: The Transformation of the Fourteenth Amendment.* (Cambridge: Harvard University Press,1977).

Bickel, Alexander M. *The Least Dangerous Branch.* (Indianapolis: Bobbs-Merrill Co., 1962).

___. *Politics and the Warren Court.* (New York: Harper & Row, 1965).

Blasi, Vincent (ed.). *The Burger Court: The Counter-Revolution that Wasn't.* (New Haven: Yale University Press, 1983).

Brown, William G. *The Life of Oliver Ellsworth.* (New York: Macmillan, 1905).

Cassidy, Lewis C. "An Evaluation of Chief Justice White", *Mississippi Law Journal,* 1938.

Carr, Robert K. *The Supreme Court and Judicial Review.* (New York: Farrar and Rinehard, 1942).

Chase, Edward. "The Burger Court, the Individual and the Criminal Process", *NYU Law Review,* 1977.

Choate, Joseph. "Choate on Fuller", *Harvard Graduate Magazine,* 1910.

Corwin, Edward. *The Doctrine of Judicial Review.* (Princeton: Princeton University Press, 1914).

Dunham, Allison and Phillip B. Kurland (eds.). *Mr. Justice.* (Chicago: University of Chicago Press, 1956).

Emerson, Thomas I. "First Amendment Doctrine and the Burger Court", *California Law Review,* 1980.

Fehrenbacher, Don E. *The Dred Scott Case.* (New York: Oxford University Press, 1978).

Frank, John P. *Marble Palace.* (New York: Alfred Knopf,1958).

___, "The Burger Court - The First Ten Years", *Law and Contemporary Problems,* 1980.

Frankfurter, Felix. *The Commerce Clause Under Marshall, Taney and Waite.* (Chapel Hill: University of North Carolina Press, 1937).

Freidman, Leon and Fred L. Israel (eds.). *The Justices of the United States Supreme Court, 1789-1978,* 5v. (New York: Chelsea House Publishers, 1969).

Graham, Fred P. *The Self-Inflicted Wound.* (New York: Macmillan, 1970).

Hart, Albert Bushnell. *Salmon P. Chase.* (Boston: Houghton, Mifflin & Co., 1899).

Hendel, Samuel. *Charles Evans Hughes and the Supreme Court.* (New York: King's Crown Press, 1951).

Highsaw, Robert Baker. *Edward Douglass White: Defender of the Conservative Faith.* (Baton Rouge: Louisiana State University Press,1981).

Hughes, Charles Evans. *The Supreme Court of the United States.* (New York: Columbia University Press, 1928).

Hyman, Harold M. and William M. Wiecek. *Equal Justice Under Law: Constitutional Development, 1835-1875.* (New York: Harper & Row, 1982).

Jay, William. *The Life of John Jay.* (New York, 1883).

Johnston, Henry P. (ed.). *The Correspondence and Public Papers of John Jay, 4v.* (New York: G.P. Putnam's Sons, 1890-1893).

King, Willard L. *Melville Weston Fuller, Chief Justice of the United States, 1888-1910.* (New York: Macmillan, 1950).

Klinkamer, Marie C. *Edward Douglass White, Chief Justice of the United States.* (Washington: Catholic University of America Press, 1943).

Konefsky, Samuel J. *Chief Justice Stone and the Supreme Court.* (New York: Macmillan, 1945).

Lankevich, George J. *The Federal Court, 1787-1801.* (New York: Associated Faculty Press,

1986).

Lee, Francis G. (ed.). *Neither Conservative nor Liberal: The Burger Court on Civil Rights and Civil Liberties.* (Melbourne, Fl: Krieger Publishing Co., 1983).

Levy, Leonard (ed.). *The Supreme Court Under Earl Warren.* (New York: Quadrangle Books, 1972).

Lewis, Walker. *Without Fear or Favor: A Biography of Chief Justice Roger Brooke Taney.* (Boston: Houghton Mifflin, 1965)

Loth, Leonard (ed.). *Chief Justice: John Marshall and the Growth of the Republic.* (New York: Norton,1949).

Mason, Alpheus Thomas. *Harlan Fiske Stone: Pillar of the Law.* (New York: Viking Press, 1956).

___. *The Supreme Court from Taft to Burger.* (Baton Rouge: Louisiana State University Press, 1979).

___. *William Howard Taft: Chief Justice.* (New York: Simon and Schuster, 1964).

McGarth, C. Peter. *Morrison R. Waite: The Triumph of Character.* (New York: Macmillan. 1963).

Meltsner, Michael. *Cruel and Unusual: The Supreme Court and Capital Punishment.* (New York: Random House, 1973).

Monaghan, Frank. *John Jay: Defender of Liberty.* (Indianapolis: Bobbs-Merrill Co., 1935).

O'Brien, David M. *Storm Center. The Supreme Court in American Politics.* (New York: Norton, 1986).

Palmer, Ben W. *Marshall and Taney: Statesmen of the Law.* (Minneapolis: University of Minnesota Press, 1937).

Powell, Jeff. "The Compleat Jeffersonian: Justice Rehnquist and Federalism", *Yale Law Journal,* 1982.

Pringle, Henry F. *Life and Times of William Howard Taft, 2v.* (New York: Farrar and Rinehard, 1965).

Pritchett, C. Herman. *Civil Liberties and the Vinson Court.* (Chicago: University of Chicago Press, 1954).

Pusey, Merlo L. *Charles Evans Hughes, 2v.* (New York: Macmillan, 1951).

Rehnquist, William H. *The Supreme Court. How it was, How it is.* (New York: Morrow, 1987).

Rodell, Fred. *Nine Men. A Political History of the Supreme Court from 1790 to 1955.* (New York: Random House, 1955).

Roettinger, Ruth L. *The Supreme Court and State Police Power.* (Washington: Public Affairs Press, 1957).

Sayler, Richard H. *et al. The Warren Court: A Critical Analysis.* (New York: Chelsea House, 1969).

Schucker, Jacob M. *The Life and Public Service of Salmon Portland Chase.* (New York: D. Appleton and Co., 1874).

Schwartz, Bernard. *Super Chief: Earl Warren and his Supreme Court.* (New York: NYU Press, 1983).

Silver, David M. *Lincoln's Supreme Court.* (Urbana: University of Illinois Press, 1956).

Smith, Charles W. *Roger B. Taney: Jacksonian Jurist.* (Chapel Hill: University of North Carolina Press, 1936).

Stites, Francis N. *John Marshall. Defender of the Constitution.* (Boston: Little Brown, 1981).

Swindler, William F. *The Constitution and Chief Justice Marshall.* (New York: Dodd, Mead and Co.,1978).

___. "The Burger Court, 1969-1979," *Kansas Law Review,* 1979.

Swisher, Carl Brent. *Roger B. Taney.* (New York: Macmillan, 1935).

Taft, William Howard. *The Anti-Trust Act and the Supreme Court.* (New York: Harper Brothers, 1914).

Trimble, Bruce R. *Chief Justice Waite: Defender of the Public Interest.* (Princeton: Princeton University Press, 1938).

Umbriet, Kenneth B. *Our Eleven Chief Justices.* (New York: Harper & Row, 1938).

Warden, Robert B. *An Account of the Private Life and Public Services of Salmon Portland Chase.* (Cincinnati: Wilstach, Baldwin and Co., 1874).

Warren, Charles. *The Supreme Court in United States History, 3v.* (Boston: Little, Brown and Co., 1923).

Warren, Earl. "Chief Justice William Howard Taft", *Yale Law Journal,* 1958.

White, Edward D. "The Supreme Court of the United States", *American Bar Association Journal,* 1921.

White, G. Edward. *Earl Warren: A Public Life.* (New York: Oxford University Press, 1982).

INDEX

Ableman v. *Booth* (1859), **5:**30
Act Concerning the District of
   Columbia (1801), **5:**90
Adams, Abigail Smith, **1:**13
Adams, John, **1:**12-13, 15, 51,
   85, 100, 118, 122, 125; **3:**7,
   12, 59, 99, 133; **4:**14, 140;
   6:9, 14
 death, **1:**85; **6:**9
 observations, **1:**11, 19, 88;
   3:94; **4:**28, 53; **5:**12, 17
 presidency, **2:**63, 68; **3:**35,
   60; **4:**89; **5:**10, 93, 98; **6:**6-7,
   89, 97, 98
Adams, John Quincy, **3:**77; **6:**2,
   14-15, 90, 98
Adams, Samuel, **1:**3, 10-11, 16,
   118, 122; **2:**12; **4:**50
Adamson Act, **5:**49
"Affair of Fort Wilson," **1:**63
Agnew, Spiro, **6:**77
Agricultural Adjustment Act,
   5:63
"Alabama claims," **5:**38
Alamance, Battle of (1771),

2:100
Alaska, **6:**37, 51
Albany Congress (1754),
   1:18
Albany Plan of Union (1754),
   2:39; **3:**1, 132
"Albany Regency," **6:**19
Alexander, Robert, **1:**123
Algeciras Conference, **6:**53
Alsop, John, **1:**122, 123
American Colonization Soci-
   ety, **6:**13
*American Communications
   Association* v. *Douds*
   (1950), **5:**67
American Independent Party,
   6:101
American Party (Know-Noth-
   ing Party), **6:**29, 99
American Relief Committee,
   6:63
American Revolution. *See* Rev-
   olutionary War
Ames, Fisher, **2:**21; **4:**12, 14, 17,
   20, 50-51, 133, 137

102